A BRIEF CATECHESIS ON
NATURE AND GRACE

HENRI DE LUBAC

A BRIEF CATECHESIS ON
NATURE AND GRACE

TRANSLATED BY
BROTHER RICHARD ARNANDEZ, F.S.C.

IGNATIUS PRESS   SAN FRANCISCO

Title of the French original:
Petite catéchèse sur Nature et Grâce
© Librairie Arthème Fayard, 1980

Cover by Victoria Hoke

With ecclesiastical approval
© Ignatius Press, San Francisco 1984
ISBN 978-0-89870-035-0
Library of Congress catalogue number 83-082108
Printed in the United States of America

CONTENTS

PREFACE

This book started as a short note, which Monsignor Philippe Delhaye, the Secretary of the International Theological Commission, had requested of the author to help the Commission in its work. The note was published later on, in July 1977, in the French language edition of the review *Communio*. We have kept the original title here because, in spite of some amplifications of a rather personal, perhaps too personal, nature, it still corresponds to our original purpose, which aimed neither at philosophical research, nor current pastoral practice, nor spiritual exhortation, but simply at catechetical instruction. This is a simple essay, undertaken to clarify a few elementary notions which lie at the roots of our faith, and which implicitly guide the day-to-day orientations of our thoughts and actions.

Nature (human nature) and the supernatural; nature (freedom) and grace; these two associated distinctions occupy a large place in traditional Catholic teaching. Today one can sometimes hear people say that both are "out-of-date". For some, this may merely be a question of semantics. But it is meaningless to claim that something is out-of-date unless one gives the reasons why. Now for anyone who wishes to remain faithful, not to some outmoded idea but quite simply to the Christian faith, all the arguments, on the contrary, show that the realities expressed by these terms are and remain fundamental. This is what we should like to explain.

I

NATURE AND THE SUPERNATURAL

1. TWO CORRELATIVE TERMS

The idea of the supernatural is as essential to
Christianity as, for instance, the ideas of creation,
revelation, the Church or sacraments. Hence, it
can be stated that it is present everywhere, not
only in the whole subsequent tradition, but from
the very beginning. William Bousset, in the early
years of this century, wrote: "Irenaeus had already
set up that complicated system of nature and grace,
that reciprocity between evolution and the supernatural, which was to prevail for so long a time in
the history of the Church."[1] We may disregard his
unfavorable opinion, as well as what may be
peculiar to Irenaeus' "system", but let us take note
of the fact itself. Indeed, we need to go back

[1] William Bousset, *Kyrios Christos: Geschichte des Christen-
glaubens von Anfängen des Christentums bis Irenaeus* (Göttingen:
Vandenhoeck and Ruprecht, 1926), 355. Cf. Philippe Bacq,
De l'ancienne à la nouvelle alliance selon saint Irénée, Le Sycomore (Namur and Paris: Lethielleux, 1978), 366.

farther still. Scripture bears witness everywhere to the idea of the supernatural.

If one wished to establish an explicit formula for it, derived from concepts borrowed from the New Testament, one could probably do so, as M. Gaston Rabeau suggested not long ago (*Introduction à la théologie*, 186), by combining the two words μυστήριον and χάρις. The Second Epistle of St. Paul to the Corinthians (1:12) also offers us an equivalent formula, at least in part: "We have behaved in the world . . . with the sincerity and grace that comes from God." And St. Peter's First Epistle invites us to long for the full development of the supernatural gift in all its plenitude on the day of the Lord's manifestation: "Set your hopes on the grace to be conferred on you when Jesus Christ appears" (1:13). [2]

When we speak of the binomial "nature—supernatural" (which should be understood as expressing both opposition between, and union of, the two terms), the word "nature" can mean either, in a more general sense, the entire universe, the whole order of creation, [3] or again, in a more particular

---

[2] It might also be observed, for instance, that the word "dogma", which was late in appearing in its strictly "dogmatic" meaning, expresses an idea which appears very clearly in the New Testament itself.

[3] In a different frame of reference one might, on the contrary, as has often been remarked, oppose the Christian

and direct sense, *human* nature; but without there being any need to cut man completely off from the universe, as was done by eclecticism in the last century, and is still done today by a certain trend in existentialism. In his recent book *Le Paradigme perdu: la nature humaine*, M. Edgar Morin (among others) has fortunately reacted against this "anthropology narrowed down to a thin psycho-cultural streamer, floating like a flying carpet over the natural universe", and he sought to withdraw the study of man from the "tiny ghetto of human sciences".[4] If, because of what makes him the "image of God", man is superior to the cosmos, he still remains nonetheless a "microcosm", just as Christian anthropology has always conceived him; and no one has shown this better in our day than Fr. Teilhard de Chardin when he gave a new impulse to this classical view through the history of life.[5]

Like the Latin word *natura*, or the earlier Greek word *physis*, this word "nature" is "one of the

---

concept of "creation" to the ancient concept of "nature" in designating the totality of the world (*cosmos*). There is no such thing as a completely univocal meaning of words.

[4] Edgar Morin, *Le Paradigme perdu: la nature humaine* (Paris: Seuil, 1974), 12, 22, 213.

[5] Many recent discoveries in the field of animal psychology, examples of which are given in the work of M. Edgar Morin, confirm Teilhard's remarks.

most elusive of all words. . . . Like a mouse stuck in tar, the mind keeps struggling with all these possible 'senses', and gets caught in the innumerable virtualities of a word with such a broad and flexible meaning."[6] So declares M. André Pellicer in his "semantic and historical study of the Latin word *natura*". Fr. Xavier Tilliette remarks, about Schelling, that this is a "ductile idea, pregnant with virtualities".[7] Jules Lachelier observed not long ago that by this same word "nature" many different things are signified which are at times opposed to each other; and yet it is not possible to seal off these connotations from each other, for they are all somehow connected; "exclusive recourse" to one or the other of these meanings "would cause the disappearance of what is really one and, at the same time, most profound" in the overall significance of the word.[8] We have here, therefore, a term possessing multiple resonances; would we not, for instance, have to make some distinction, simplifying again, between the

[6] André Pellicer, *"Natura": Etude sémantique et historique du mot latin* (Paris: P. U. F., 1966), chap. 1. See also Robert Lenoble, *Esquisse d'une histoire de l'idée de nature* (Albin Michel, 1969).

[7] Xavier Tilliette, in *Studi urbineti* (1977), 391.

[8] *Vocabulaire de la Société française de philosophie*, 5th ed. (1947), distinguishes eleven different meanings of the word.

"nature" of a scholar and that of a philosopher or that of a poet?[9] It is a term which must be employed judiciously, but—as everyday use proves—one that we can hardly do without, in spite of the difficulties it causes. Even after the severest warnings against it, it always comes right back to hand.

In its theological use, however (the only one which interests us here), the word does not offer great difficulty. For it is then a purely *correlative* term which consequently can be properly understood only in its relationship with the other term "supernatural". "Anything that does not derive from divine adoption in man, even if it does derive from the spirit and liberty in him, can be called natural."[10] Consequently, employed in this connection, the word does not suppose any systematic philosophy, nor does it imply too narrow an idea of the nature in question. It is in no way opposed to the notion of man considered primarily, for

[9] Cf. M. Barthélemy-Madaule, *Lamarck, ou le mythe du précurseur* (Paris: Seuil, 1979), chap. 2, 39–62: "La Nature".

[10] G. Martelet, *Victoire sur la mort: éléments d'anthropologie chrétienne* (Lyons: Chronique sociale de France, 1962), 127–28. Cf. Karl Rahner, *Questions théologiques aujourd'hui*, trans. Gélébart (Brussels and Paris: DDB, 1965), vol. 2, 36: "Raising man to the supernatural level is the absolute fulfillment—although totally gratuitous—of a being that cannot be 'defined', that is, 'delimited' as nonhuman beings are, because he is a spirit and a transcendence towards the absolute Being."

instance, as person, or as liberty, or as spirit, or as history, or even as existence, according to the terminology recently adopted by Claude Bruaire.[11] No more is it opposed to "culture", since culture is, on the contrary, something proper to human nature which, whatever the circumstances, is specifically "human", radically different from all other natures, living or inanimate, found in the cosmos.[12] Let us merely observe that, in any case, it is impossible to exclude the whole idea of nature when studying the human being. "Man is that being whose norm is nature, but who goes beyond nature. Yes; but can he do this entirely?"[13] He cannot simply be reduced to "nature", and this has been pointed out in this century by theories as diverse as phenomenology, personalism and existentialism, as well as by a whole branch of marxism.[14] Man, therefore, cannot be content merely

[11] Claude Bruaire, *Une Ethique pour la médecine* (Paris: Fayard, 1978).

[12] Cf. my study of *Le Mystère du surnaturel* (Paris: Aubier-Montaigne, 1965); M.-J. Nicolas, O.P., "L'Idée de nature chez saint Thomas", in *Revue thomiste* (1974; republished by Téqui, 1979).

[13] Claude Bruaire, *L'Affirmation de Dieu* (Paris: Seuil, 1964), 11. Cf. Morin, *Le Paradigme perdu*, 101 and 221: "Man is a natural being by his culture." "Man's nature is not opposed to his history, nor is man's history opposed to his nature."

[14] A. Dondeyne, *Foi chrétienne et pensée contemporaine*

to "follow nature" because it offers him nothing normative—but neither can he simply "struggle against nature", "as though he himself were in no way biological but was entirely a creature of culture".[15] His task is rather to "welcome" it in order to transform it.

All these remarks may seem perfectly obvious. Still, it may not be superfluous to remind ourselves of them today. For, as Jeanne Hersch remarks, we are passing through

> a strange epoch. On the one hand, we claim to reject all the natural and social data proper to our condition and to replace them by arbitrary decrees in the name of the rights of the human person. But on the other hand, wherever it would be advisable for us to convey and embody our values in the concrete reality actually given to us, we hesitate to make the decisions, we replace them with declarations, necessities and laws.[16]

Again, sometimes "modern man, be he marxist or

(Louvain, 1951); idem, "Education religieuse et monde moderne", in *Lumen Vitae* 12 (Brussels, 1957), idem, "L'Historicité dans la philosophie contemporaine", in *Revue philosophique de Louvain* 54 (1966).

[15] Alain Cugno, *Saint Jean de la Croix* (Paris: Fayard, 1979), 175–77.

[16] Jeanne Hersch, *L'Homme est mort–qui le DIT?* (n.d.).

technocrat, falsely imagines that through his technology he can wield an unlimited sway over nature
and create his own history."[17] Then sometimes he
abdicates, and goes so far as to speak of his own
"death", in the name of the very sciences and
technology which reduce him to an inextricable
knot of natural relationships.

We need to turn away from these two extreme
positions. If we take them unilaterally, none of
the terms we have cited can suffice to define man;
none is free from many ambiguities. M. Maurice
Blondel showed, for instance, the inadequacies
of personalist views, even those of profoundly
Christian inspiration; for they leave out the "cosmic
preparation" and hence lack the substructure of
natural metaphysics.[18] Maurice Nédoncelle did as

---

[17] Gaston Fessard, S.J., *Libre méditation sur un message de Pie
XII*, Christmas 1956 (Plon, 1957), 27. Cf. E. Schillebeeckx,
Approches théologiques (Brussels and Paris: Editions du C. E. P.,
1967), vol. 3, 135–36: "In this era of science and technology,
the world . . . is now nature humanized by man's labor; it
manifests the glory of man who makes it, or the shadow of
man who destroys it. . . . Now that it is only mere raw
material in the hands of man the creator . . . nature is the
work of man. . . . Man goes forward triumphantly to encounter nature, and his technological power forces it to bow
before him."

[18] Maurice Blondel, "Les Equivoques du personnalisme",
in *Politique* 8 (March, 1934): 193–205; idem, *L'Etre et les êtres*
(Alcan, 1935), 272–85.

much in the 1962 preface to his work on *Personne humaine et nature*. Long ago Maximus the Confessor, to cite only him, sought to bring out the basic connection between the nature and the person in the human being.[19] But when, on the other hand, a theologian noisily greets as a "discovery of modern anthropology" the growing perception that man "cannot be considered as a *thing* ordered by nature towards an end", but that he is "a free agent set in a given situation, who must organize his existence according to a scheme, a concept of life", one can conclude both that through this false dilemma the author is freeing himself with ease from a caricature that has nothing to do with the most traditional Christian anthropology, and that he is playing dangerously with the word "nature".

For, on the one hand, if there really is a fundamental affirmation at the basis of Christian anthropology, it is certainly "that man is the image of God; that he cannot be reduced to being a mere atom in universal nature or an anonymous element in the human race", as John Paul II recalled in his speech at Puebla, referring to the Constitution *Gaudium et spes* of Vatican II.[20] Before this, in his book *Amour et responsabilité* (*Love and Responsibility*),

---

[19] On the anthropology of Maximus, see J. M. Garrigues, *Maxime le Confesseur: la charité, avenir divin de l'homme* (Paris: Beauchesne, 1976), pt. 1.

[20] *Gaudium et spes*, 12, 3; 14, 2.

Monsignor Karol Wojtyla had drawn on the most classical tradition to show that it is impossible to "reduce to a mere biological order that can be modified as the individual wishes, what is in reality the very order of existence, subject to personalistic norms."[21] It really is not against an obsolete notion rooted in the Bible and Christianity (no matter what one person or another may have thought), but on the contrary against a new naturalism that "phenomenology, existentialism and marxism considered as dialectic materialism" have sought to react, in a common desire to set aside "the various attempts at making man just a slice of nature, a simple moment in cosmic evolution."[22] On the other hand, it seems to us a piece of sophistry to scent "naturalism" or "thing-ism" in every explanation of man in which the word "nature" appears. Did not St. Leo the Great exclaim, in his celebrated apostrophe: "O man, awaken! Know the dignity of thy nature; remember that thou wert made in God's own image!"[23]

---

[21] Preface to the French edition (1965), 8: "No one, after reading this book carefully, will again be able to indulge in those facile diatribes, those caricatural pamphlets against the traditional theses, which dishonor even some of our Catholic publications."

[22] Dondeyne, *Foi chrétienne*.

[23] *"Expergiscere, o homo, et dignitatem tuae cognosce naturae.*

Certainly, this is not to say that philosophical reflection has not made any real progress in throwing light on the characteristics of the human being, as displayed most concretely in man's response to God's call. The work of Fr. Gaston Fessard has given us the analyses we needed concerning man considered as a historical being and as a free agent; but he was able to do this only by analyzing at the same time the principal essential categories of human *nature*.[24] Romano Guardini has sketched a dialectic of nature and culture, from which it is apparent that "there is no such thing as pure culture"; and that, beyond a certain limit, "culture can outrun genuine humanity and become inhuman", as a warning instinct makes us feel.[25] After showing that man is "spirit, free and time-bound" and consequently a "historical being" and not simply "a well-defined essence endowed with

---

Recordare te factum ad imaginem Dei. . .": *In Nativitate Domini*, sermo 7, 2, PL 54, 267–68.

[24] G. Fessard, especially *De l'actualité historique*, 2 vols. (Brussels and Paris: DDB, 1960), and *La Dialectique des Exercices spirituels de saint Ignace de Loyola*, Théologie 35 and 66 (Paris: Aubier-Montaigne, 1956 and 1966). On the various meanings of the word "nature" in Marx, see the profound analyses by the same author in *France, prends garde de perdre ta liberté* (Paris: Témoignage chrétien, 1946) 139–45 and 153–59.

[25] Romano Guardini, *Christianisme et culture*, trans. Gwenendael (Casterman, 1967), esp. 194–211.

a principle of specific operations", that he is not "ready-made, but makes himself by his choices, by projecting what he wants to be", Fr. Marcel Régnier, without claiming to have made any discoveries, concludes that the "progress in awareness" which has helped us understand these things better is progress indeed, but "progress in the knowledge of human *nature*".[26]

As for the correlative of human nature, namely, the "supernatural", the word, taken in the technical sense which alone belongs to it here, appears only rather late in the language of Latin theology, and even later in ecclesiastical documents. I believe it occurred for the first time in 1567, in St. Pius V's Bull condemning Baius, (propositions 21 and 23). What the term designates is not so much God or the order of divine things considered in itself, in its pure transcendence, as, in a general and as yet indeterminate manner, the divine order considered in its relationship of opposition to, and of union with, the human order.

To deny this fundamental distinction, if one truly understands what it means, to deny it regardless of the words in which it is expressed,

---

[26] M. Régnier, "L'Homme, nature ou histoire?" in *Etudes* 329 (1968): 447–50; in the text cited above, the italics are mine. See also my *Pic de la Mirandole* (Paris: Aubier-Montaigne, 1974).

would be to deny as well and in its very principle every notion of revelation, mystery, divine Incarnation, redemption or salvation. That would be to deny the Christian faith itself. One might, after that, still profess a sort of deism, as did Voltaire and the other leaders of the "Enlightenment", or as did Jean-Jacques Rousseau in his somewhat more religious manner;[27] one would not necessarily fall into an atheistic naturalism;[28] one might maintain, as many did in the nineteenth century, a

[27] Henri Gouhier, *Les Méditations métaphysiques de Jean-Jacques Rousseau* (Vrin, 1970), chap. 1: "Nature et histoire dans la pensée de J.-J. Rousseau"; André Ravier, "Le Dieu de Rousseau et le christianisme", in *Archives de philosophie* 41 (1978): 353–434.

[28] Exaltation of the idea of nature is common to the majority of the philosophers and writers of the eighteenth century, to Diderot as well as to Voltaire, to Rousseau as well as to Lessing, Herder and even Deschamps—each one, of course, understanding it in his own way. Strangely enough, the renewed admiration for that century which had "nature" as its battle cry ("This was the master idea of the century", says Paul Hazard) coincides today, and often in the works of the same authors, with a bitter and often unenlightened criticism of the idea of human nature that has been defended by the Catholic Church. For historical information, cf. Paul Hazard, *La Pensée européenne au XVIIIᵉ siècle* (Boivin, 1946), vol. 1, 151–73; Jean Ehrard, *L'Idée de nature en France dans la première moitié du XVIIIᵉ siècle*, 2 vols. (Paris: S. E. V. P. E. N., 1963).

sort of theism which admitted the idea of a certain kind of Providence and gave evidence of Christian origin in more than one way. Nowadays, such beliefs are less attractive than some form of pure immanentism or of a self-professed radical humanism. All are conceptions, in any case, that disfigure man himself. Embracing them, one would no longer believe in the living God who reveals himself to man, who intervenes in man's history, who "became man so that man might become God". One would no longer believe in the God of Israel, the God of Scripture and of Christian tradition, the God of Jesus Christ, the God, one and three, whom we acknowledge in our Credo.

2. THE TRUE SUPERNATURAL

Sometimes, indeed often, the idea of the supernatural has been confused with that of miracles, which are called "supernatural effects". It has even been confused with the idea of the action contrived by some god as a sort of "expedient", as has often been repeated by some, echoing Bonhoeffer. But this was never the idea taught by a "prescientific" Christianity, no matter what many persons claim. Never, in the authorized tradition of the Church, do we find any "proof of the existence of God" established on such a basis;

the simplest seminary manual, the most elementary modern catechisms are, as a rule, as silent on this point as are the Gospels, the ancient Fathers of the Church, the medieval theologians and the great Christian spiritual writers of all centuries. True, after the event, people who believed in God "the Creator of heaven and earth", in God "the Father of our Lord Jesus Christ" and "our Father", may very often, out of ignorance or superstition or mere laziness, have attributed to his direct intervention, apart from any "secondary cause", certain "marvels" which they were unable to explain in any other way. That is a different question. Maine de Biran, who was no despiser of the Christian faith, correctly criticized "that indolent philosophy which, in the moral as well as the physical world, sees a miracle in every phenomenon which it does not feel capable of explaining."[29] Observations of this kind, which are in no way opposed to the Christian idea of miracles, are even less opposed, one might say, to the idea of the supernatural.

[29] Pierre Maine de Biran, "Examen critique des opinions de M. de Bonald" (1818), on the subject of the origin of language. (Unpublished by the author, but published by Ernest Naville in *Maine de Biran, sa vie et ses pensées* [Paris: J. Cherbuliez, 1857], vol. 3, 244.)

Further mistakes have been made by putting this idea in the same category with that other, often highly suspect, idea of extraordinary mystical phenomena, or with that of gifts which, "super-added" to man by his Creator, would have wrested him from his specific finality in order to allow him access to a higher one, which in this sense could be called "supernatural". In these two last cases, as in the case of miracles, classical theology used the more correct term "preternatural".

This variety of acceptations for the word "supernatural", still taken in the very general meaning of "transcendental", and which has occasioned such great confusion, often arises from mistakes made by unbelievers misinformed about Catholic doctrine. Or it may be a question of adventitious meanings, more or less based on analogy, and as such more or less legitimate. Again, it may be the result of the elaboration of certain systems occurring late in Western theology, systems that the Christian Orient never knew. These theories, unknown to both the Greek and the Latin Fathers, and which began to take shape only at the dawn of modern times, were organized around the idea of "pure nature" conceived of as having a "purely natural" end. Yet these theories were never universally accepted in the West, and were unknown or denied both by the majority of Orthodox theologians and by the Christian philosophers of modern Russia.[30] The least one can say of them is that they do not command assent from the Christian faith. Heinrich Schlier explained this very well in a few words, based on data found in the New Testament: "It is because God from the beginning made himself man's end, by presenting himself to man as his salvation; and it is because he first set man in motion towards that end that man's essence and existence were given their determination."[31]

Any human word can undergo various extensions of its analogical meaning. And any human word can suffer from certain inconveniences. Not one exists which cannot be misunderstood. So, let us begin by spelling out what we do not mean by

[30] See also Olivier Clément, *Le Christ: terre des vivants* (Bégrolles en Mauges, France: Abbaye de Bellefontaine, 1976), 73 and 136. Cf. below, Appendix A.

[31] Heinrich Schlier, "L'Homme d'après la prédication primitive", in *Essais sur le Nouveau Testament*, trans. A. Liefooghe (Paris: Cerf, 1968), 133–34. On this subject one may or may not agree with Karl Rahner that there is a "supernatural existential" which results from man's vocation to be an adoptive son of God; this existential would be the resonance of the divine call within the depths of man's nature. I do not see much use in imagining such an *ens rationis*. The quotation from Schlier seems to me more felicitous in its simplicity; but I do not wish to enter into details of this kind here.

"supernatural", in order the better to understand what it actually does mean.

The supernatural is certainly not the *abnormal* in the sense that a miracle is. Yet it is more marvellous than the miracle, and its achievement lies much farther beyond the *powers* of our human nature than a miracle surpasses the powers of the physical agents found in material nature. Nor is the supernatural something *adventitious*, something "super-added" such as may have been the "supernatural gifts" attributed to man while he was still in the state of innocence; yet it "dignifies"[32] man much more than these did; it raises him much higher still above the level of his own *essence*, since it is entirely out of proportion with that essence. Finally, the supernatural must not be defined solely by its characteristic of *gratuitousness*; and yet it is infinitely more gratuitous than any other kind of favor could possibly be, and infinitely surpasses the *necessities* of any possible nature. In this triple sense it fully deserves its name.[33]

Christian language uses another term to designate this reality: a scriptural, especially Pauline term, one which has remained in the Greek tradition: the word πνευματικός (from *pneuma*, spirit).

[32] This is the word which is dear to the Scotists.

[33] Henri de Lubac, *Surnaturel: études historiques*, Théologie 8 (Paris: Aubier-Montaigne, 1946), 428.

A Christian is one who has received "the first fruits of the Spirit".[34] In some ways this term might even seem preferable. It has the great advantage, important in Christian anthropology, of marking a distinction from ψυχικός (psychic, *animalis*).[35] We can scarcely do without this word if we wish to explain that the "longing for God", which is basic to man, must not be understood as a "psychic" desire—while at the same time avoiding the epithet "transcendental" which, because of its philosophical origin, might give rise to more than one ambiguity. But besides the fact that Scripture obliges us to distinguish between man's *pneuma* and God's, the word, in the present case, is inconvenient because it remains too indeterminate, both in Latin and in our modern languages. Of itself, it does not refer to the *pneuma* any more than to the νοῦς; nor does it, of itself, suggest the idea of a fruit produced by the Spirit of God, of a divine reality. One can understand "spiritual" in a very ordinary sense, as synonymous with immaterial. That is why the word "supernatural", consecrated

[34] Rom 8:23. Cf. Vatican II, Constitution *Gaudium et spes*, I, 4.

[35] I sketched the history of this tradition, starting with St. Paul, in my book *Mistica e mistero cristiano* (Milan: Jaca Book, 1979), 59–166: "L'Antropologia tripartita nella tradizione cristiana".

by long usage, would seem to be hard to replace when precision is called for. It too, of course, has its disadvantages; it may have encouraged simplistic theories and have been given doubtful interpretations in Catholic theology as well as in the "supranaturalism" found in some Protestant traditions[36] or in a more recent literary tradition that runs back to Victor Hugo[37] and leads to "surrealism". As we said, without explanation no word enables us to avoid all pitfalls. Yet, until the English language disappears from our universe, we shall be able to repeat with Pascal: "From all material objects taken together no one can ever extract the tiniest thought. That is impossible; it is something belonging to a different order. Out of all material objects and all spirit no one can ever draw a movement of true charity; that too is

---

[36] The word has always been sparingly used in French. Renan mentions it and uses it to designate what had been "brought low by the criticisms of the new German school": "M. Feuerbach et la nouvelle école hégélienne", in *Etudes d'histoire religieuse*, 2nd ed. (Paris: M. Lévy frères, 1857), 416–17.

[37] Defining the "complete poet", Hugo said: "For humanity and nature, vision is observation; for supernaturalism, vision is intuition". Quoted by Claude Pichois, *Littérature française* (1979), vol. 2, 423.

impossible; it belongs to a different order, the supernatural order."[38]

"It belongs to a different order." That is the decisive word, which demolishes the pretention of eliminating the supernatural in the name of scientific progress. Alongside this passage from Pascal, let us cite some lines written by Renan in his youth, in *L'Avenir de la science*.

> . . . Science is worthwhile only in so far as it can seek and discern what revelation claims to teach. . . . I do not need . . . to prove that there is a contradiction between science and revelation; for me it suffices that they both tell the same story. . . . I conceive of pure science, science which understands its purpose and its aim, only outside of all supernatural belief. . . . Belief in a revelation, in a supernatural order, is the negation of criticism, a relic of the old anthropomorphic conception of the world, formed at a time when man had not yet acquired a clear idea of the laws of

[38] Cf. de Lubac, *Surnaturel*, 428. Another passage from Pascal where our word is found gives it a different title of nobility: "If everything is subjected to reason, our religion will have no more mystery, nothing supernatural. If the principles of reason are violated, our religion will be absurd and ridiculous:" *Pensées*, in *Oeuvres complètes*, ed. Jacques Chevalier, 4th ed., Bibliothèque de la pléiade (Paris: Gallimard, 1954), 1089.

nature. . . . It is not just one line of reasoning, but the whole of modern science that yields this tremendous result: there is no such thing as the supernatural. . . . The task of modern thought will be completed only when belief in the supernatural, in whatever form, is destroyed.[39]

Renan never got over this delusion of his early years. He returns to it at length in his preface to the thirteenth edition of his _Vie de Jésus_, where he fails to distinguish what is "beyond science" from what is "against science"; he turns aside from everything that lies outside the sphere of empiricism and condemns indiscriminately miracles, transcendence and mystery. "By the very fact", he wrote, "that one admits the supernatural, one has left the domain of science. . . . There is no reason to believe in something of which the world offers no perceptible trace." Now what he wrote in 1848 and in 1864 still expresses the convictions of a number of our contemporaries, more than ever dyed-in-the-wool partisans of a scientism which has long since lost its romantic colorations but whose reign, thanks to the development of "human sciences" and to the prodigious progress

[39] Renan, _L'Avenir de la science: pensées de 1848_, 1st ed. (Calmann-Lévy, 1890), 39, 42–43, 46–48.

made by technology, seems to them to be still continuing.

But all progress has its set-backs. Our humanity, in a certain number of its select representatives, has gone ahead on a path which leads it to narrow the scope of its intelligence. To devote itself entirely to its task of exploration, this group has renounced every dimension other than that of experimental research. To it, any metaphysical concern seems vain, lacking in good sense and out-of-date. And it brings into every other field of inquiry the habits acquired in its conquering march; its very successes put blinders on it; and when it comes up against "a different order" of reality, it tries to brush this aside as a chimera and falls a victim to a fundamental *ignoratio elenchi*.

"One can carry natural science as far as one likes", observed M. Etienne Gilson;[40] "it will never reach the supernatural"—just as, even if Gagarin had flown a thousand times farther up into space, he still would never have met God. This is why the scientist, as such, cannot even conceive of it as a hypothesis. But in addition, as Pascal warned us, the supernatural order is different

[40] Etienne Gilson, *Le Philosophe et la théologie* (Vrin, 1968), 185

from and more than a trans-empirical and transcendental order that escapes scientific investigation; for "that which lies beyond the empirical is not for that reason beyond nature and humanity."[41] In other words, between our human nature and our destiny there lies an "infinite disproportion". One cannot move from man to God "by walking forward on the same level, so to speak"; the abyss between them can be bridged only "by the marvellous invention of divine charity". In its theological meaning, whose precision is necessary here, "the supernatural is proposed to us as an entirely gratuitous relationship, one which, so to speak, is totally 'un-naturalizable' ".[42]

The following section will explain this by looking into another refinement of the classical vocabulary.

[41] Maurice Blondel, in *Etudes philosophiques* 6 (1931): 3–5.

[42] Maurice Blondel [Bernard de Sailly], in *Annales de philosophie chrétienne* (July, 1907), 346–47: "It is revealed to us as a reality inaccessible to the grasp of all human consciousness, all natural perception . . . an inviolable secret of the divine Being, the inner life of the mysterious Trinity. . . ." Quoted by Claude Tresmontant, *La Crise moderniste* (Paris: Seuil, 1979), 234. On the history of Blondel's thinking on this subject see the analyses in Raymond Saint-Jean, S.J., *L'Apologétique philosophique: Blondel, 1893–1913*, Théologie 67 (Paris: Aubier-Montaigne, 1966).

3. ADJECTIVE OR NOUN?

The reader may have noticed that the distinction drawn above seems somewhat awkward; on the one hand we use a noun, "nature", and on the other an adjective, "supernatural". The nouns "supernature" (in Latin *supernatura*) and "super-essence" (*supersubstantia*) were rarely used in ancient theology, and only to indicate the very being of God; so we read in a text by the Cistercian, Isaac of Stella: "*cum de Dei ineffabilis supernatura aut verbo loqui cogimur qui silere non sinimus.*"[43] It was only recently, during the nineteenth century, that certain authors (Scheeben in particular, following Suárez, was one of the earliest)[44] began to speak regularly of "nature" and "supernature", thus completing in their language a deviation of thought whose history was already long. The change can be found even in translations. Thus, when Newman wrote: "When we are called to what is supernatural", an excellent French translator made him say: "When we are called to a supernature". Worse yet, in a reputable theological reference work in its English

[43] *In Sexagesimam* G, PL 194, 1768 B; cf. 1755 B: *super-substantia*. These words come from Denys.

[44] French translation of his *Dogma* (Palmé, 1881), vol. 3, 411, no. 594, etc.

edition we find: "The supernatural (or, preferably, 'supernature')". It is true that it immediately adds "since it is not an entity", so that the deviation seems to be purely grammatical, as is also the case in this reflection of Dr. Paul Chauchard about man "formed in the image of God, whose nature is made to be exalted by a supernature."[45] The fact remains that this new terminology, which in our century has become more and more encroaching and is taken by some—even some "Thomists"—as a *tessera orthodoxiae*, has certainly made the traditional doctrine more obscure, and even falsified it. Let us say at the very least that it was the sign and the effect of the doctrine's being obscured, and by that very fact has contributed to discrediting the doctrine itself. In reality, what we have here is not (as a decadent theology supposed in the not very distant past) two juxtaposed realities (two "natures"), or, if one prefers, two realities the

[45] Paul Chauchard, *L'Etre humain selon Teilhard de Chardin* (Paris: Librairie Lecoffre, 1959), 11. Since once a custom has been introduced it is followed more or less by everybody, it can happen that good authors whose competence is undeniable use the word "supernature" in a way that was formerly incorrect. We can see this here and there even in the writings of M. Etienne Gilson, in his analyses, which are indeed very precise, of St. Thomas' thought. Cf. his work *Le Thomisme*, 5th ed. (Vrin, 1945), 496. The same thing is true of Blondel and of many others.

second of which would be superimposed on the other, while both remained exterior to each other. It is not a question of two substantial natures, incapable of copenetrating each other, one of which would override the other—or, as taught by extreme Lutheranism and Jansenism, the first actually suppressing or suffocating or mutilating the other in order to reign in its stead.

Several authors have taken pains to bring this out very explicitly. One is Fr. Karl Rahner, in his somewhat contorted explanations whose general meaning is nevertheless clear.[46] More recently Fr. A. M. Dubarle, O.P., pointed out to us that it would be useless to seek anywhere in Scripture "for the source of the later theological teaching that distinguished two ends for man: one natural, proportionate to the capacities of his essential nature; the other supernatural, presupposing a gratuitous and more radical elevation of his nature and his faculties of knowing and willing." "We

[46] Karl Rahner, *Mission et grâce*, trans. Charles Muller (Paris and Tours: Mame, 1962), vol. 1, 65–67: "Grace is essentially a determination, an elevation and a divinization of nature. . . . Let us not therefore imagine it as though it were a higher story that the heavenly architect in his wisdom would have added to the bottom one (nature) in such a way that the lower floor, keeping intact the structure which belongs to it as such, would merely be a support to this upper one. . . ."

must, then", he remarked, "clearly distinguish between two usages of the double category: natural and supernatural. . . . One cannot go from the one to the other without precautions."[47] In more general terms Fr. Yves Congar had already written in 1951: "The idea of a supernature added to nature . . . is a Western one; it is the result of that malady of analysis and separation characteristic of the Western mind."[48] It is the malady of a late Western mentality (still rampant as ever among clergymen, but it attacks others also), a malady which for many centuries was unknown to both Latins and Greeks; it did not affect the great theologians of the Middle Ages,[49] and even today some have managed to remain immune to it. But it has provided a pretext for exhibiting the Christian faith in a false light.[50] It is also reproached with

[47] A.-M. Dubarle, O.P., *La Manifestation naturelle de Dieu d'après l'Ecriture* (Paris: Cerf, 1976), 241–42. This is the final conclusion of the work.

[48] Yves Congar in *Irenikon* (1951), 309–10.

[49] To mention only two recent examples, the doctrine of St. Thomas Aquinas which had remained obscure for a long time has been restored to its true meaning by two recent articles: S. Dock, O.P., "Du désir naturel de voir l'essence divine d'après St. Thomas", in *Archives de philosophie* (Jan.–March, 1964); and S. Pinckaers, O.P., "Le Désir naturel de Dieu", in *Nova et Vetera* (1977).

[50] Cf. Léon Brunschwigg, *Vraie et fausse conversion* (Paris:

arbitrarily supposing the existence of a "shadow world". Full of ambiguities, this last notion is brandished as something to frighten people with, especially since a new tidal wave of Nietzschean conformism has begun to roll over us.[51]

Latin theology's return to a more authentic tradition has taken place—not without some jolts, of course—in the course of the last century. We must admit that the main impulse for this return came from a philosopher, Maurice Blondel. His thinking was not primarily exercised in the areas proper to the professional theologians, nor did it base itself on a renewed history of tradition. Still, he is the one who launched the decisive attack on the dualist theory which was destroying Christian thought. Time after time he demonstrated the deficiencies of the thesis of the "extrinsicist" school, which recognized

---

P. U. F., 1951), 138–39. The author thinks he is describing the classical theology of the Church when he speaks of the "Thomistic syncretism in which the mediation of angelic substances sustains the common edifice of nature and of supernature". Neither St. Thomas nor any other theologian considers this "mediation" the passage to the supernatural.

[51] The "Kingdom of God" is not a "world". It is not to be classed with this world; its relationship with the latter is one of *"radical heterogeneity"*. Cf. Cugno, *Saint Jean de la Croix*, 178–83.

no other link between nature and supernature than an ideal juxtaposition of elements which . . . were impenetrable to each other, and which were brought together by our intellectual obedience, so that the supernatural can subsist only if it remains extrinsic to the natural and if it is proposed from without as something important only in so far as it is a supernature. . . .[52]

Then, attacking in turn both of these "monophorisms", he overcame the opposition between an extrinsicism which ruined Christian thought and an immanentism which ruined the objective mystery which nourishes this thought. It was mainly because of his influence, as Fr. Henri Bouillard explained, that "we have consciously ceased to conceive of the natural and the supernatural orders as though they were two superposed storeys without any inner connections",[53] and a

[52] Maurice Blondel, *Histoire et dogme* (La Chapelle-Montligeon, France: Librairie de Montligeon, 1904), chap. 3, 67; idem, *Exigences philosophiques du christianisme* (Paris: P. U. F., 1950); idem [Testis], articles for the Semaine sociale de Bordeaux et le monophorisme, in *Annales de philosophie chrétienne* (1909–1910), 57f.

[53] Cf. Jean Guitton, "Existe-t-il une nature humaine?" in *Semaine des intellectuels catholiques* (1950): "Henceforth, we avoid representing grace under an architectural image, like a bell tower which would rise above and cap an edifice already complete in itself; and this is why some people are uneasy with the word *surnature*, which seems to suggest a *supernature*

concern for avoiding such a conception has even led more than one theologian in recent times to "restrain as much as possible the use of these terms."[54] At any rate, today it would be tilting at a ghost, or at best attacking a corpse crumbling into dust, to sally forth as G. Vahanian did in 1977 against "the believer who is still mentally cloistered in the walls of the supernatural", who must "feel that he belongs to two different worlds" and consequently would be torn apart in his innermost being by this "dichotomy". "It only takes a flick of a finger", continues Vahanian, "to bring down the whole construct of these two worlds, natural and supernatural."[55] A late scholastic theology may have built that construct, but it has already crumbled, and it never was, we repeat, the teaching of the great Catholic tradition.[56]

All this, however, is not to say that the distinc-

---

artificially added. Today, rather than this older image we prefer analogies drawn from life, and particularly from impregnation. . . ." The only fault one can find with this passage is that it gives the impression that the image and the words criticized were "ancient", whereas they were in fact modern.

[54] Henri Bouillard, in *Bulletin de la Société française de philosophie* (Jan. 25, 1975), 14.

[55] G. Vahanian, *Dieu et l'utopie* (Paris: Cerf, 1977), 30 and 42.

[56] Cf. Rahner, *Questions théologiques*, vol. 2, 22: "The theology of the Middle Ages had deeper and richer ideas about uncreated grace than we do."

tion between (human) nature and the supernatural must now disappear.[57] If there exists a "correspondence", a "certain profound identity between the logic of human existence and the internal logic of Christian history", the affirmation "of a natural desire for the supernatural has the merit of suggesting this correspondence." In times like these, when philosophers and theologians often experience a similar desire to get down to the concrete right away, one can certainly say that, just as the word *nature* "fails to indicate clearly the logic of freedom, so too the word *supernatural* does not fully express the reality of the communication that God makes of himself in Jesus Christ." These words, therefore, do not suffice to express the "personal and historic relationship" in which "the Christian mystery" consists.[58] However, in our opinion there would be more than one difficulty in trying to eliminate their use completely. They oblige us, in our theological reflections, to proceed step by step. They remain useful because "they

[57] Vahanian seems to perceive this himself, for he writes (*Dieu et l'utopie*, 104) as though to excuse himself: ". . . We are not trying by this bias to get back to the ancient dichotomy of the natural and the supernatural."

[58] Henri Bouillard, "L'Idée de surnaturel et le mystère chrétien", in *L'Homme devant Dieu*, Théologie 58 (Paris: Aubier-Montaigne, 1964), vol. 3, 153–66.

forewarn us against the temptation of 'naturalizing'
the mystery", in other words, "of undervaluing
the divine Love which freely evoked another
love."[59]

4. *ADMIRABILE COMMERCIUM*

The supernatural, one might say, is that divine
element which man's effort cannot reach (no self-
divinization!) but which unites itself to man,
"elevating" him as our classical theology used to
put it, and as Vatican II still says (*Lumen Gentium*,
2), penetrating him in order to divinize him, and
thus becoming as it were an attribute of the "new
man" described by St. Paul. While it remains
forever "un-naturalizable", it profoundly penetrates the depths of man's being. In short, it is
what the old Scholastics and especially St. Thomas
Aquinas called (using a word borrowed from
Aristotle which has often been completely misunderstood) an "accidental form" or an "accident".[60] Call it an accident, or call it a *habitus*, or
"created grace": these are all different ways of

[59] Ibid., 166.

[60] St. Thomas Aquinas, *Summa Theologica* I–II, q. 110, a.
2: "*Utrum gratia sit qualitas animae*", and ad 2: "*Quia gratia est
supra naturam humanam, non potest esse quod sit substantia aut
forma substantialis, sed est forma accidentalis ipsius animae. . . .*"

saying (even if one thinks they need various correctives or precisions) that man becomes in truth a sharer in the divine nature (*divinae consortes naturae*; θείας κοινωνοὶ φύσεως: 2 Pet 1:4). We do not need to conceive of it as a sort of entity separated from its Source, something like cooled lava—which man would appropriate to himself. On the contrary, we wish to affirm by these words that the influx of God's Spirit does not remain external to man; that without any commingling of natures it really leaves its mark *on* our nature and becomes in us a principle of life. This Scholastic notion of created grace, so often belittled today, does express the incontrovertible fact that "it is we, ourselves, and our creaturely being, which the active presence in us of the Spirit makes divine, without for that reason absorbing us and annihilating us in God."[61]

St. Thomas Aquinas speaks of a "connaturality" established between God and man. In classical theological language this has two names:

One is an objective name and denotes the reality in itself, and this is grace, which is a sharing in God's own intimate reality; as "sanctifying grace" it gives us objectively a share in God's being; as

[61] Louis Bouyer, *Le Père invisible* (Paris: Cerf, 1976), 288. Cf. Rahner, *Questions théologiques*, vol. 2, 28–29.

"actual grace" it enables us to live this reality and act with it. The other name is subjective and shows our consciousness of its presence; it is divine virtue (i.e., an aptitude, a capacity to turn ourselves towards God) and is thus the triad: faith, hope and charity.[62]

At another level, and in different language, St. Bernard likewise suggested the two complementary truths which, demanding acceptance by our faith, arouse our grateful admiration. It is in the difference—or as we would say today, more expressively, in the distance—always maintained between one being and another, and above all between the creature and its Creator, that the most intimate union is brought about between them. It is a relationship of reciprocity in unity, and its perfect model is found in the circumincession of the three Persons of the Trinity. Let us listen to St. Bernard himself in one of his sermons on the Song of Songs. First he stresses, so as to avoid all confusion and to forestall all ὕβρις on our part: "*Non plane pari ubertate fluunt amans et Amor, anima*

---

[62] Hans Urs von Balthasar, *De l'intégration: aspects d'une théologie de l'histoire*, French trans. Bourboulon et al. (Brussels and Paris: DDB, 1970), 106: "This 'trinity' bespeaks a unique attitude having three aspects. . . . These three aspects must not be placed . . . on parallel lines; they form, rather, a circle in which they mutually enrich each other."

et Verbum, sponsa et Sponsus, Creator et creatura . . . sitiens et Fons"; and yet, he continues, the reciprocity in unity is total; for, in fact, "*etsi minus diligit creatura, quoniam minor est, tamen si ex tota se diligit, nihil deest ubi totum est.*"[63]

That paradox, the fruit of the "admirable exchange" (*admirabile commercium*) established once for all by the Incarnation of the Word of God, which Bernard sought to express in his ardent and image-laden lyricism, is what the language of the Schoolmen succeeded in compressing into a unique formula, abstract and dry in appearance and less accessible to our current mentality which has passed through existentialism and personalism. Its full significance emerges only in the light of the entire organic complex.[64]

---

[63] St. Bernard, *In Cantica*, sermo 83, no. 6, *Opera*, ed. Jean Leclercq (Rome, 1957), vol. 2, 302: "Although the creature loves less, since it is lesser, still, if it loves with its whole self, nothing will be wanting there where all is found."

[64] This, it seems to me, is exactly what Antoine Vergote is trying to say when he tells us that "the saving power of the Spirit consists in naturalizing God in the human spirit and in divinizing the latter through the divine immanence": "L'Esprit, puissance de salut et de santé spirituelle", in *Experience de l'Esprit: mélanges Schillebeeckx*, eds. Paul Brand et al. (Paris: Beauchesne, 1976), 223. M. Nédoncelle suggested that we call this a "heterogeneous identity": *Personne humaine et nature* (Paris: Aubier-Montaigne, 1963), 14–15.

One must indeed admit that the original meaning of the formula had rather quickly faded out of the Scholastic tradition itself, even in those schools which did not deny it outright. It ended by wearing out, just as the relief of a medal or coin wears out. This is the story of what happens in the course of time to many theories, many concepts which had sprung from a correct and profound spiritual insight. And even now we must make a slight historical effort to avoid attributing to these authors the contrary of what they actually intended. Here the main author is St. Thomas Aquinas himself, a young genius who did not fear to oppose a trend of thought that had gone off in a wrong direction, yet which had behind it the authority, already solidly established, of Peter Lombard, the "Master of Sentences". For St. Thomas, as Fr. Louis Bouyer explains,

the soul . . . will find its completeness and go beyond itself in God. Disagreeing with Peter Lombard, in fact, he would not admit that grace is purely and simply the gift of the Holy Spirit, of the Third Person of the Trinity as it is in itself . . . . He realized that if such were indeed the case, man would certainly be the temple of the Spirit, but not God's living temple, vivified by the presence of its Guest who assimilates our life to his divine life. The uncreated grace of the gift of the

Spirit, according to him, has its prolongation in the soul itself in created grace, i.e., a divine quality that assimilates the soul to God and makes it share in his own life.[65]

Later, as Fr. Bouyer goes on to say, this doctrine

was often misunderstood and even interpreted exactly contrary to what it actually meant. Because grace is called "created" some argued that it must be a second nature, superimposed on our original nature, a "supernature". Nothing could be more contrary to the deep conviction of St. Thomas. If grace, as he conceives it, is created, it is created in the soul. This means (he says so explicitly) that it is not a superior and distinct nature added to the soul as a sort of cloak. It is a quality infused into the soul.

Grace is supernatural in the fundamental sense that it is superior to any created or creatable nature, but it is in no sense a "supernature". It is, so to speak, a new "accident", "hidden in and penetrating the substance of the soul and rendering it, as a soul, capable of living God's own life, his divine life."[66]

Let us also make an effort, if this be necessary,

[65] Louis Bouyer, *Introduction à la vie spirituelle* (Desclée, 1960), 154–55.
[66] Ibid.

to realize the capital importance, from the point of view of our destiny, of a discussion such as this which, to a superficial observer, may appear as nothing but a tangle of subtleties, mostly out-of-date. In spite of the word "accident", which makes some cry out against "Aristotelianism", i.e., a revolution of thought which is supposed to have corrupted the spirit of Christianity and from which we must strive to free ourselves completely, not only to regain our footing alongside contemporary culture but also to get back to authentic Christian vigor, let us admit that this doctrine elaborated by Thomas Aquinas was in fact a revival of the tradition of the first centuries, which without a doubt had its source in the Gospel and in St. Paul. This doctrine expressed in its own language "the paradox of this Spirit, who is the Spirit of God, but who becomes the spirit of the soul."[67] Origen, that penetrating interpreter of St. Paul's teaching about the *pneuma*, had written long ago that "in every creature, holiness is accidental."[68]

[67] Ibid.
[68] Origen, *Peri Archôn*, 1.5, 5, Koetschau 5, 77 (PG 11, 164 C). Cf. Hans Urs von Balthasar, *Origène, esprit et feu*, French trans. (Paris: Cerf, 1959), vol. 1, 97–100, giving a resumé of Origen's doctrine on this point; also de Lubac, *Mistica e mistero cristiano*, 77–84.

5. A DISTINCTION WHICH REMAINS

Setting aside a terminology so worn-out and now so badly understood by some modern Scholastic writers as well as by many critical minds outside of the Church, Maurice Blondel succeeded, without becoming esoteric, in giving new life to the old doctrine which will always remain the basis of our hope. He did this in particularly apt terms, in a manuscript published posthumously. There he explains that the supernatural "is not an arbitrary 'something extra', a form extrinsic to man. . . . It is an adoption, an assimilation, an incorporation, a consortium, a transformation which, through the bond of charity, insures both the union and the distinction of two incommensurables"; and again, the supernatural is not "a sort of distinct being, a receptacle into which we are to be absorbed, emptying us of our human nature; it is on the contrary intended to be in us, *in nobis*, without ever being on that account something coming from us, *ex nobis*."[69] And according to Fr. Teilhard de Chardin, on this point more correct and more

[69] Maurice Blondel, *Exigences philosophiques du christianisme* (Paris: P. U. F., 1950), 58 and 162. On the history of this volume, see René Virgoulay and Claude Troisfontaines, *Maurice Blondel: bibliographie analytique et critique* (Louvain, 1975), vol. 1, 173–74.

traditional than many Scholastics in his time, at least in the clarity of his view: "The supernatural is a ferment, a soul, not a complete organism; it comes to transform 'nature'."[70]

Let us keep in mind this word "transformation", so dear to Teilhard de Chardin as well as to St. Paul, and which from the beginning played an essential role in the formulation of the Christian mystery.[71] We shall find it again further on, along with some others which complete it. For now, let us be content to say, in summing up, that the pair "nature-supernatural", as we have explained it, must be thought of at the outset as a relationship of opposition, of spiritual otherness and of infinite distance; but that if man so wills, it resolves itself finally in an association of intimate union. We have here, as Blondel remarks,

> both the distinction and the reciprocal copene-
> tration of Pascal's "orders". It is not enough to
> show their opposition to each other; we must
> bring them together, *in eodem dramate*. . . . Be-
> tween the two gifts a dynamic continuity exists,
> and an intelligible relationship.[72]

[70] Pierre Teilhard de Chardin, *Le Milieu divin* (Paris: Seuil, 1957), 199.

[71] Cf. Henri de Lubac, *La Pensée religieuse du Père Teilhard de Chardin* (Paris: Aubier-Montaigne, 1962), chap. 12: "La Transfiguration du cosmos", 185–94.

[72] Blondel, *Exigences philosophiques*, 256–57.

It is, as the ancient writers liked to put it, the twofold relation of the *datum optimum* of creation to the *donum perfectum* of divinization.[73]

Such a relationship expresses at one and the same time both the divine transcendence, the gratuity of the gift God makes of himself, the "grace", and also the deep realism of the quality of "children of God" which is won for men in principle by the Incarnation of the Word: "ὅσοι δὲ ἔλαβον αὐτόν, ἔδωκεν αὐτοῖς ἐξουσίαν τέκνα θεοῦ γενέσθαι. . .".[74] Teilhard de Chardin liked to use the word "physicism" to suggest this real quality of grace, as a reaction against the saccharine theories then called "moral" which were popular during his youth.[75] It is one of the essential characteristics of all Christian mysticism.[76]

---

[73] I explained this in *Le Mystère du surnaturel*. See especially chap. 5, 105–33.

[74] "All those who did welcome him he empowered to become the children of God": Jn 1:12.

[75] Cf. for instance Maurice Blondel and Pierre Teilhard de Chardin, *Correspondance commentée*, ed. Henri de Lubac, Bibliothèque des archives de philosophie 1 (Paris: Beauchesne, 1965), 57–59. The words "physical" and "organic" are commonly used by him in opposition to "moral" or "juridical".

[76] The best word for expressing this idea, if one hesitates to use the traditional vocabulary, might be the word "charism", as St. Paul seems to understand it in chapters 5 and 6 of the Epistle to the Romans; but unfortunately an inveterate use,

It is nothing new that in different contexts of thought and under varying terminologies men have rejected the *supernatural*, as thus defined; it is not only its counterfeits that they reject, nor have they done so because of some misunderstanding. Some have deliberately decided to limit themselves to the realm of empirical man, within our earthly and restricted horizon, considering any more far-reaching ambition illusory. Others have presumed to divinize themselves by virtue of some internal power or seed.[77] Still others have felt that the mass of human individuals was destined to be joined with the divine essence of humanity at the term of history, or merely to prepare for this, after some kind of dialectic evolution. Such had already been, for instance, in the early centuries of our era, the claim of certain "pseudo-gnostic" sects combatted by Irenaeus, Clement, Origen, Didymus, etc.[78] And throughout the history of the Church this

---

which might be considered regrettable, has reserved this word to designate certain gifts, both extraordinary in their manifestation and not sanctifying to the individual, such as the "charism of healing" mentioned in chapter 12 of the First Epistle to the Corinthians, verses 9 and 30.

[77] Concerning interpretations of St. John of the Cross, cf. Henri Bouillard, "La 'Sagesse mystique' selon saint Jean de la Croix", in *Recherches de science religieuse* 50 (1962): 481–529.

[78] Cf. de Lubac, *Le Mystère du surnaturel*, 115–16.

was also the temptation that assailed more than one Christian who plunged into some sort of native interiority, beyond all Christian or even moral activity. This was the interpretation that some historians sometimes wished to give to the doctrine taught by genuine saints, making of what these said about man divinized by grace an affirmation of his divinity by essence. But for anyone who wishes to be a true Christian, who knows that he is a "son by adoption",[79] the reality expressed in the classical distinction between nature and supernatural (no matter what words one may wish to use in describing it, if better ones can be found) is not any more "out-of-date" or "worn-out" today than it was in the second, the thirteenth or the sixteenth century of our era.

One pamphleteer wrote recently in this connection: "So, here we are, back again at this venerable theological distinction between nature and grace; one really has a right to ask how our Christian thinkers can accommodate themselves to this theological schizophrenia." One may think that when he allowed the imposing word "schizophrenia" to slip from his pen like a bugbear, the author really did not know what he was saying (as though everything that is not confused were

[79] Cf. Gal 4:5.

schizophrenic), or that he had not made the slightest effort to understand this "venerable distinction" he was poking fun at, or that he could not imagine, in spite of the lessons taught by history, what turning aside from this kind of "schizophrenia" can do to threaten human liberty.[80] Perhaps he was prejudiced against the Christian faith. That quotation, which has little originality about it, at least shows us that it is not inopportune to explain the simplest notions over and over again, even at the risk of appearing boring, over-long, scholastic and pedantic.

"For the simplest believer, the orientation towards the supernatural should characterize 'his conception of man and of freedom', as well as that of nature and of history, and consequently should 'govern contemporary thinking', just as it does that of all times."[81]

[80] Cf. my *Méditation sur l'Eglise*, 2nd ed. (Paris: Aubier-Montaigne, 1953), chap. 5: "L'Eglise au milieu du monde", 139–73.

[81] Gaston Fessard, *Chrétiens marxistes et théologie de la libération*, Le Sycomore (Namur and Paris: Lethielleux, 1978), 167.

II

CONSEQUENCES

Nature and the supernatural: from this first fundamental distinction there follow a certain number
of consequences. It will be good for us to remind
ourselves of some of them now.

1. HUMILITY

First of all, this distinction brings out the importance of humility in the Christian life. We must
not understand it merely as a moral virtue, but
as a fundamental disposition upon which the entire
edifice rests. Speaking of "man's divinization
through grace" Fr. Teilhard de Chardin rightly
remarked: "This is more than a simple union; it is
a process of transformation during which all that
human activity can do is prepare itself, and accept,
humbly."[1] Put in another way—we need not be

[1] Pierre Teilhard de Chardin, *Le Milieu mystique: ecrits du
temps de la guerre* (Grasset, 1965), 161–62.

afraid of words—humility is a *passive* virtue: it is a readiness to accept what is born "not of blood, nor of the flesh, nor of man's will";[2] a readiness to welcome God "who comes down".[3]

A historical-phenomenological analysis would show that a disposition of this kind had no equivalent in what we have been accustomed to call classical antiquity.[4] One can find there certain "impressive" moral virtues, "with the sole exception of humility. For the ancient mind this virtue was merely despicable, something base and servile."[5] The Greeks, for instance, had indeed some inkling of mildness, expressed by the adjective πρᾶος; but when using this word, after the example of the

---

[2] Jn 1:13.

[3] Eph 4:9–10. This text from St. Paul is the one which Fr. Teilhard loved most. He himself often stressed the idea of "descent": "the flame that descends"; "the rays descending from the heart of God"; "from him all descends", etc. Cf. "Descente et montée dans l'oeuvre du Père Teilhard de Chardin", in Maurice Blondel and Pierre Teilhard de Chardin, *Correspondance commentée*, ed. Henri de Lubac, Bibliothèque des archives de philosophie 1 (Paris: Beauchesne, 1965), 127–53, where many other examples will be found.

[4] Cf. Pierre Adnès, *Dictionnaire de spiritualité* (Paris: Beauchesne, 1969), 47, 1156–87; Henri de Lubac, *La Foi chrétienne*, 2nd ed. (Paris: Aubier-Montaigne, 1970), 318–19.

[5] P. Régamey, O.P., *Ce que croyait Dominique* (Paris and Tours: Mame, 1978), 167.

Greek versions of the Old Testament which had already assimilated it to ταπεινός (humble) the Gospel gives it an entirely different scope. As they become part of the language of Christianity, the Greek words take on "a new meaning, infinitely stronger and more demanding". By the same token, the Greek ideal seems "limited and paltry". Never would the ancient Greeks have dreamed of recommending humility to anyone. It is a "complete moral revolution" which took place, following upon Christ's revelation and upon the realization of what the mystery of the Incarnation meant.[6]

Humility is no less absent to the various other forms of paganism, whether refined or gross. Nor do we find it in the great spiritual systems of India, or in those of the Far East. In Buddhism, for instance, in some of its spiritual teachers, one can note signs of pride (there is no other word in our language which adequately describes them) which are not in the least considered as blemishes—quite

[6] Jacqueline de Romilly, *La Douceur dans la pensée grecque* (Belles Lettres, 1979), 309–14; cf. 320. Let us note with Fr. Schillebeeckx that "in paganism what we find is not pride properly speaking, but rather the absence of any Christian humility": *Approches théologiques* (Brussels and Paris: Editions du C. E. P., 1967), vol. 3, 83, with a quote from André Bremond: "Classical paganism . . . is expectant".

the contrary. We know too that Victor Segalen, a man of rare intellectual refinement who embraced Taoism, defined himself as "the arrogant mystic".[7]

Humility, which is essentially evangelical and Pauline, is a characteristic of the "Christian condition". It is contrary to the "spirit of the world", using this term in its pejorative sense. It was not by chance that Paul, when urging the Christian to conform his sentiments to those of Christ, reminded him that the latter "emptied himself" (ἐταπείνωσεν ἑαυτὸν);[8] nor was it by chance that the First Epistle of John describes the quintessence of the spirit of the world as "pride of life".[9] Charles Péguy had a profound intuition of this. Christianity, he wrote, "made of humility something more than a virtue; its very mode and rhythm, its secret savor, its external yet intimate attitude both carnal and spiritual, its situation, its way of life, its continual experience, almost its very being."[10]

[7] Letter to Yvonne V. S., June 13, 1909. Quoted by Bernard Hué, in *Littérature et arts de l'Orient dans l'oeuvre de Paul Claudel* (1914), 270.

[8] Philemon 2:8.

[9] 1 Jn 2:16.

[10] Charles Péguy, "Un Nouveau Théologien", in *Oeuvres en prose, 1898–1914*, ed. Marcel Péguy, Bibliothèque de la pléiade 114 and 122, 2 vols. (Paris: Gallimard, 1957), vol. 2, 1066.

This Christian humility, the natural wellspring of prayer, is first of all, of course, quite opposed to any "metaphysics of self-sufficiency"; it recognizes our condition as creatures, i.e., our "radical incompleteness"; this is radical, fundamental humility, one might say, something as spontaneous as breathing itself. It "consists in accepting that individual reason is ruled by eternal reason". In fact, far from all ὕβρις, this humility instead of abasing the human creature really establishes its grandeur, if it be true that in each of us our intellect is a reflection of the face of God. Yet it clashes with that desire for total autonomy which in our day expresses itself more than ever before by the claim to "invent the world" and to "create one's own values out of nothing".[11] Humility contradicts not only the ideology of pagan antiquity, but also a certain "modernity" that is frequently described as "humanism", as though it had some sort of monopoly over that word, and which is a "rejection of God". Marx, Nietzsche and Sartre are its most famous representatives. Nietzsche was the first to speak explicitly of "creating one's values"; of course, for him these are not mere

[11] Joseph Ratzinger, "Je crois en Dieu", in the anthology *Je crois: explication du symbole des Apôtres*, trans. L. Jeanneret, Le Sycomore (Paris: Lethielleux, 1978).

"imaginary concepts", but "realities inseparable from the beings which create and reveal them", i.e., those supermen from whom he hopes that a regenerated world, superior to our present humanity, will issue forth. For Sartre, on the contrary, who understood quite well that universal and absolute values cannot exist outside of a divine consciousness, and who rejected such a consciousness, every man can create his own values at will, but these have no more consistency than the arbitrariness of his liberty.[12]

In this way the humility which consists in accepting being is replaced by another very different kind of humility that could be described as "the disesteem for being", for it supposes that in himself "man is nothing but some kind of animal, come from nobody knows where or how, whose

[12] So, remarks J. Beaufret, the system proposed in *L'Etre et le néant* "is neither more nor less than an inversion of Christian theology. The God who created being out of nothing is replaced by man, the creator of nothingness in the midst of being": *Introduction aux philosophies de l'existence* (Denoël-Gonthier, 1971), 92; quoted by Yves Labbé, *Humanisme et théologie* (Paris: Cerf, 1975), 57. Cf. Mme. J. Parain-Vial, "L'Homme peut-il créer des valeurs?" in *L'Astrolabe* 511 (March–April, 1978): 11–17. The author shows how this "modern" notion of value destroys every idea of truth and every concept of the good and reproduces the sophism of Callicles demolished by Socrates in the *Gorgias*.

silhouette remains unfinished",[13] and about which no firm reference allows one to say that one is "worth" more than another. But by leading man to accept his condition as a creature, Christian humility, which is the basis of a "humanism" that does not run the risk of degenerating into an "anti-humanism", at the same time makes him recognize that in the creation of the "new man", just as in the creation of the natural man, God is still the one at work.[14] One might add that this humility molds itself on the image of "God's humility", for he, although sovereignly free in his transcendence, makes himself partially immanent in his creatures by that *kenosis*, that "excentration", that "movement of descent" which is the Word's Incarnation.[15]

[13] Ratzinger, "Je crois en Dieu".

[14] Claude Tresmontant, *La Mystique chrétienne et l'avenir de l'homme* (Paris: Seuil, 1977), chap. 6: "Ontologie et théorie de la connaissance", 179–82.

[15] Just as the "missions" of the divine Persons reproduce, in some free manner outside of the Trinity, their internal "processions", it has been possible to speak of a still more radical humility on God's part, a humility native to his eternal being and consisting in the excentration (ecstasy) of each Person sharing himself completely with the other two. . . . Still, if such attempts at explanation are to be legitimate, one must not forget their analogical character, and one should suggest them without forgetting the respect due to the mystery of the divinity. See below, part II of this chapter.

Discussing the change that took place in the history of Italian painting between the time of Fra Angelico and that of Masaccio or Piero della Francesca, André Malraux observed, with a penetrating insight, that "by this loss of humility, no matter what other Christian sentiments may remain, the depths of Christianity itself have disappeared."[16]

Paul VI reminded us of this in 1976 at one of his general audiences: "The humility we are speaking of", he remarked,

> is not that moral virtue which St. Thomas placed in the domain of temperance, even though he recognized that it held a privileged place in the wider field of moral living in general.[17] It is a virtue which addresses itself to the fundamental truth of our religious relationships, to the essential reality of things. It places in the first rank the existence of a personal God, all powerful and omnipresent, who takes the first step towards man. It is the humility of the most Blessed Virgin

[16] Maurice Clavel quotes these words in "Le Légendaire du siècle", *Le Nouvel Observateur* (May 12, 1976). Clavel also says (in *Ce que je crois* [Grasset, 1975], 307): "Everyone has a choice between pride and humility, between the will to power and poverty of spirit."

[17] Cf. *Summa Theologica* II–II, a. 5.

in the Magnificat that enables the creature to
understand itself in its total dependence on God. . . .
The logic of the Gospel is inspired by this humility
of Christ, the One who is both God and man, a
humility central to the Christmas mystery.[18]

No one in Christian tradition has formulated this
teaching more constantly or with more felicitous
expressions than St. Augustine. He places on Jesus'
lips the words: *"Humilis veni, humilitatem docere
veni, magister humilitatis veni."* "O wondrous
exchange", he comments in his *Confessions*,[19]
"eternal life is promised to us by the humility
of the Lord, who bowed himself down to our
pride." As for the edifice erected on this foundation
alone, it can be described briefly by the celebrated
triple expression of St. Paul referred to above:
πίστις, ἐλπίς, ἀγάπη (faith, hope and charity)
which all of Christian tradition has made its own,
and which Pascal, in the spirit of St. Paul himself,
condensed still further into the "greatest" of the
three (μείζων: 1 Cor 13:13): charity. In the thir-

[18] Audience of November 29, 1976, in *Documentation
catholique* (Jan. 16, 1977), 58.

[19] Augustine, *Confessions*, bk. 1, chap. 9, 17. Cf. *In Joannem*,
tract. 25, 15, etc. On the spirit of evangelical humility see Jean
Daniélou, *Contemplation: croissance de l'Eglise*, Communio
(Paris: Fayard, 1977), 107–9.

teenth chapter of his Gospel, in his solemn proclamation of the love "even unto the end" and the
account of the washing of the Apostles' feet, St.
John brought together the foundation and the
pinnacle in an indissoluble unity.[20]

Let us bring this section to a close by citing these
beautiful lines from Milosz' "Cantique de la
connaissance":

> I speak only to those minds which have acknowl-
> edged that prayer is the first of man's duties.
>
> The most exalted virtues: charity, chastity,
> sacrifice, knowledge, even the love of the Father,
>
> Will not be credited save to those who, by their
> own free choice, have recognized the absolute
> necessity of humbling themselves in prayer.

---

[20] On humility and charity, see the teaching of Cassian, of
the "Rule of the Master" and of St. Benedict, in Adalbert de
Vogüé, *La Règle de saint Benoît* (Paris: Cerf, 1977), chap. 7,
171–83. On "the three that remain" see Dom Marc-François
Lacan in *Recherches de science religieuse* 46 (1958): 321–43; Hans
Urs von Balthasar, *La Foi du Christ* (Paris: Aubier-Montaigne,
1968), 62–67: "In a different, more immediately apparent
sense, it is clear that faith disappears when vision comes."
One can specify that charity can no more be reduced to mere
orthopraxis (correct conduct) than faith can be reduced to
orthodoxy (correct belief). The summit and the basis correspond: Christian charity, like Christian humility, is not a
simple moral virtue. Both of them "belong to a different
order, the supernatural order".

2. MYSTERY

Another consequence: if it is true that the last end of man, his destiny, his vocation, is "supernatural", that it transcends anything that might be attained by human efforts, or might result from mere human history, then it should surprise no one if the revelation thereof should be characterized permanently by the presence of *mystery*. It is and will always remain in this world "that which eye has not seen, ear has not heard, the heart of man has never conceived."[21] This is not only the doctrine taught by the sublimest mystics, it is the teaching of the Church, who addresses herself to all. She lays down this inviolable rule: "*Inter creatorem et creaturam non potest similitudo notari, quin inter eos major sit dissimilitudo notanda*."[22] The same doctrine was reiterated in 1870 by the First Vatican Council which reminded certain rash theologians that God will always be "*super omnia quae praeter ipsum sunt vel concipi possunt ineffabiliter excelsus*."[23] The humblest catechesis cannot but echo this.

[21] Cf. 1 Cor 2:9.

[22] Fourth Lateran Council.

[23] Constitution *Dei Filius* (in *Denzinger-Schönmetzer*, 1963), chap. 1, 587: "God is infinitely elevated above all that exists or can be conceived apart from him."

The situation here is indeed different from that of the object of human science. The latter's ever-conquering activity, its multifaceted research, cause the frontiers of the unknown, of the unexplored territory, to draw back—even if it gets lost in blind alleys at times, even if each of its discoveries is superceded by the next one, even if it knows in advance that it will never come to the end of its tasks because the unknown, the unexplored, appears ever more vast the further progress takes us. The object of faith is quite different. It can never be subjected to reason either by the intuitions of a genial intellect or by a collective effort, or even by history's slow maturing. Christian faith can be—and history shows that it was indeed—the promoter of reason;[24] but it is not, itself, a science or a revealed philosophy; such expressions are devoid of meaning. To use Pascal's words again, it belongs *to a different order*.

This does not mean that faith does not have a light proper to itself,[25] nor that it completely lacks all rational justification, nor (and this is the point

[24] Cf. Etienne Gilson's writings on the problem of "Christian philosophy"; and my own *Recherches dans la foi*, Bibliothèque des archives de philosophie 27 (Paris: Beauchesne, 1979).

[25] ". . . *Nova mentis nostrae oculis lux tuae claritatis infulsit*": Preface of the Mass of Christmas.

which interests us here) that it excludes all objectivization. On the contrary; from the beginning—
and it could not have been otherwise—Christian
faith spontaneously expressed itself in symbols
and concepts; the abundant richness of the texts of
the New Testament bear witness to this. Very
soon it became necessary to conceptualize its object
in more precise fashion, so as to maintain correctly
its true scope in the minds of believers. From this
there followed dogmatic formulas; their notions,
although more fully worked out, are evidently
not exhaustive. Their indispensable role, far from
reducing or "encapsulating" or violating the mys-
teries, is on the contrary to protect them against
the constantly renewed attempts to seize hold of
the mystery so as to imprison it in unchanging
human constructs.[26] Our Fathers in the faith, the
main authors of the great trinitarian and chris-
tological definitions, were above all wary of a
sacrilegious "curiosity".[27] One makes a great

[26] See for instance Jean Stern, "Le Dogme chez Newman",
in *Axes* (Feb.–May, 1976), 53–62.

[27] On the meaning of *curiositas* and *scrutatio* in questions of
faith, see Henri de Lubac, *Exégèse médiévale* (Paris: Aubier-
Montaigne, 1961), vol. 3, chap. 4, sec. 2: "Les Mamelles trop
pressées". In principle, says Anastasius of Sinai, before and
after many others, *"non est Ecclesiae necessaria et utilis, eorum
quae a Deo sunt absconsa scrutatio et manifestatio"*: *In Hexameron*,

mistake in imagining that the intense labor which
led to the texts of Nicea, Ephesus or Chalcedon
was inspired by a desire to go beyond the simplicity
of the Scriptures, or even to adapt the expression
of Christianity to a given "cultural milieu" other
than its original one, at the risk of "hellenizing"
the faith received from the first Christians—in
other words, to speak frankly, and as today they
are so wrongfully accused of having done, at the
risk of altering the faith's substance by adapting it
to profane categories. *A fortiori*, never did they
have in mind anything resembling this decultur-
ization and this systematic inculturization of the
faith that some theoreticians have invented, as
though this faith, in order to migrate from one
culture to another, supposedly sealed off from one
another, had to die in order, nobody knows how,
to be reborn again. . . .[28] The facts were just the

8, PG 89, 2971–72. Cf. Henri de Lubac, *La Foi chrétienne*,
278–306.

[28] Furthermore, at the same time, far from considering
this primitive faith as some sort of cultural phenomenon
which had to be carefully kept apart from any other culture—
which would have meant locking themselves into an impossible ghetto and betraying the universal character of the truth
received from Christ—those whom we so rightly call the
"Fathers of the Church", our Fathers in the faith, "caused the
Gospel message to permeate their own respective cultures
(mainly Greek and Latin, but also Syriac, Coptic, Armenian)".

opposite: the constant struggle was to protect and preserve the faith. The word "consubstantial" at Nicea, the union of the two natures at Chalcedon, marked the triumph of the primitive faith against the attacks of a hellenism that sought to engulf it. *Non in te me mutabis, sed tu mutaberis in me.*

To wish to limit oneself strictly to biblical formulas in explaining the faith is a snare. *Scriptura sola* may have been brandished like a battle flag at one time; it still remains an untenable position, in fact as well as in principle. The ancients were not deceived. Not only did the faith of the Church precede all the writings of the New Testament and guide the reinterpretation of the Old Testament—our faith is not a "religion of the book", and these writings are anything but a manual or a code—but one cannot fail to inquire about the meaning of

---

But in doing so they did not attempt to "liberate" this message from its original "Hebraic" culture. "On the contrary, they tirelessly translated, commented on and assimilated that message despite the fact that its language and its logic (its 'philosophy' as they called it) could have been repellent to disciples of the Greek philosophers and rhetoricians. That was how they became 'Fathers', because for the first time an effort was made to transmit Israel's heritage to all nations. They 'originated' the Church; and in addition, almost without intending to, they originated a renaissance of their own cultures", which some might have accused them of destroying (P. Aucagne).

formulas, to compare them with one another, to juxtapose them, assimilate them. . . . Now, if one disregards the necessarily abstract precisions laid down by the Councils, how will one avoid the deviations and perversions due to the invasion of "hellenism" which these clarifications were supposed to correct? No one perhaps has said it better than Karl Barth who observed with pointed irony that the more a theologian wishes to be considered a pure biblicist, disdaining the Church, her dogma and tradition, the more surely he ends "in absolute dependence upon the spirit of the times."[29]

On the other hand, there is also an indispensable effort to understand the faith. St. Augustine went so far as to say: "*Fides, si non cogitatur, nulla est*".[30] The human mind is made in such a way that it cannot hold to a truth, cannot maintain it, unless it seeks and seeks continually. Calling a halt to thought would mean death. But, as we have said, the development of scientific research is one thing, that of philosophic reflection is another and that of believing thought is something different still. This last, whatever its characteristics—and we know

[29] In his *Théologie protestante au XIXᵉ siècle* (French trans. L. Jeanneret [Geneva, 1969]), Barth observes this and explains it with reference to Menken (318–22), to Hofman (401–2), to Beck (408–10) and to Kohlbrügge (426); see also 321.

[30] Augustine, *De Praedestinatione Sanctorum*, 5, PL 44, 969.

that it does not proceed in the same way for an Origen, an Augustine, a Bernard or a Thomas Aquinas[31]—will always operate within the parameters of the faith itself which, in the unity of its object, will always remain inclusive.

The unique mystery to which it adheres may come to be grasped in greater depth, but never surpassed. It is always within the realm of the "defined", as Claudel said, that we shall have to "plunge", but only in order "to seek the inexhaustible there".[32]

When we are dealing with human research there exist no "pillars of Hercules" anywhere to obstruct the path.[33] But here the spatiotemporal metaphor of "going further" has no application. The symbolic formulas in which our faith is expressed are not, like literary allegories, an imaginative reformulation of simple human ideas, fashioned after the event, which reason in its infancy might not at first have been able to grasp in any other way. Hence these formulas cannot be left behind some day by a reason which supposedly has

[31] Cf. de Lubac, *Recherches dans la foi*, 93–111.

[32] Paul Claudel, *Oeuvres en prose*, eds. Charles Galpérine and Jacques Petit, Bibliothèque de la pléiade 179 (Paris: Gallimard, 1965), 424.

[33] Cf. Auguste Valensin, "L'Ulysse dantesque", in *Regards sur Dante* (Paris: Aubier-Montaigne, 1956), 175–94.

reached its maturity, like clouds which the depart-
ing airplane pierces through in order to sail on into
the zone of pure light. The rationalist imagines
that he is breaking through the obscure layer of
symbolism, where his ancestors had remained
imprisoned, in order to gaze directly on the sun[34]
(unless he pretends, sometimes, to have invented
this sun itself in order to shed light on the clear
idea which he has conceived). On the contrary,
because he is animated by the Spirit, the Christian
knows that no word having a human origin is
truly adequate to express the divine newness to
which he is invited, the first fruits of which he has
received.[35] He knows that no idea conceived and
expressed by him, however strict its normative
formulation may be so as not to allow it to go
astray, can be fully commensurate. He recognizes
at the same time both the objectivity of the knowledge guaranteed by the tradition of the Church[36]
and the innate inadequacy of his present mode
of knowing. For every statement of the faith is

[34] "There is a more youthful and more powerful force",
Vigny has Libanius say in *Daphné*, "which consists in com-
prehending the divinity . . . without the gross use of symbols."

[35] Rom 8:14, 23.

[36] Without which, as Newman remarks, every proposi-
tion, even for instance "God is love", can lead to the worst
aberrations. Cf. Stern, "Le Dogme chez Newman", 55.

twofold; as regards us it necessarily consists of two views, the two apparent objects of which seem at first glance to be opposed to each other, not to say contradictory. These two views tend to coalesce at an infinite distance upon a single object, but the intuition of this unity escapes us. This is why the coherent plenitude after which we aspire can never, in our present condition, be anything but an aspiration. "It will be given to us", writes the Russian theologian Paul Florenski, "only by him who will wash the creature clean from all her impurities, by the Holy Spirit. . . . Antinomies are a constitutive element in religion, considered as something intellectual. Thesis and antithesis, like warp and woof, make up the cloth of religious experience."[37] In his profession of faith Maurice Clavel not long ago told us something similar: "It is our condition which splits up the one Reality into all these various truths; and the locus and link of all these divisions is our history. . . . There are obviously no dogmas in paradise."[38]

In paradise, yes; but in our earthly condition

[37] Paul Florenski, *La Colonne et le fondement de la vérité*, 1st ed. 1914, French trans. Constantine Andronikof (Lausanne, 1975), 110–11. As Bossuet said, we must hold fast to "the two ends of the chain".

[38] Clavel, *Ce que je crois*, 266–67.

concepts and definitions remain indispensable to mark out the route for us. The dogmas which they express are "the beginning, the point of contact in us of the infinite verities whose full and deepest meaning is reserved for eternity."[39] To wish to emancipate oneself from these, or to pretend to have left them behind, or to treat them as approximations which one may correct as one likes, would be to devote oneself to deviation. To translate by negative concepts, in the normal exercise of one's intelligence, that which may have been a suspension of concepts in an instant's experience, or what will be their hoped-for disappearance in eternal light, would be the effect of a gross paralogism. Let no one try to discover in the preceding lines any trace of some subtle anti-intellectualism, nor even a preference for a negative theology.[40]

---

[39] Pierre Charles, S.J., "Le Scandale de la foi", in *Nouvelle revue théologique* (1946), 369–90; reprinted in *L'Eglise sacrement du monde*, Museum Lessianum section théologique 55 (Belgium: Desclée de Brouwer, 1960), 37–56. See Hans Urs von Balthasar, *Catholique* (Paris: Fayard, 1976), 104: "Definitions surround the mystery like cherubim with their flaming swords."

[40] I stated my position on this topic, even as regards the "natural" knowledge of God, in my book *Sur les chemins de Dieu* (Paris: Aubier-Montaigne, 1956). See especially chaps. 2 and 5.

It is normal and right that a meditation rising towards the Absolute from the being met with in this world (τὰ ὄντα) should apprehend the latter at its summit as nonbeing (apophatic language), in order to bring out the infinite qualitative distance. But when this meditation is on the word of revelation which comes down from God, it is right that the totally different being of Love, in its majesty which subjugates the soul, should make use of cataphatic language (positive, affirmative) and should relegate us to a silence of faith and adoration. Then within this silence we can—above all by the grace of God—hear something, and to some extent understand it. In the incarnate Word all this becomes evident, and all apophatic language on his part becomes impossible.[41]

The distrust, or rather the rejection, which the believing soul displays when faced by the undertakings of a reason which seeks to eliminate mystery is not only the fruit of an elementary reflection on the data furnished by faith as well as on the nature and the conditions of our intelligence; it is the necessary, vital reaction against all forms of *gnosis* which seek to take possession of Christian truth, to embrace it, to "seize" it, and in so doing betray it. Nothing more surely leads one to mis-

[41] Hans Urs von Balthasar, *Une Méditation catholique*, French trans. in *Axes* (June–July, 1979), 30, note 4.

interpret Christianity than the claim to "understand" it. *"Quidquid scientia comprehenditur, scientis
comprehensione finitur."*[42] The effort of our intelligence, which recognizes no limits, does not lead
to our mastering Christianity, but on the contrary
to our plunging, with a better realization of what
we are doing, into its mystery. Unity takes place
in the night. Of the truest realities, the most
definitive things, the only ones which shed some
light for us on this opaque world and give us some
explanation of ourselves, we see only, St. Paul
tells us, *per speculum et in aenigmate.*[43] This dull
mirror is a prism which necessarily breaks up the
divine light for our eyes and presents it to us
in enigmas. The reason is that in this world
we are still only "a certain beginning of the new
creature".[44] No doubt, as Florenski also observes,
it can happen that "through the wide cracks in
human reason we can sometimes catch a glimpse
of the blue sky of eternity."[45] But this is never
anything but an imperfect and fleeting anticipation.
"We hope for that which we do not see."[46] Thus,
for as long as our history lasts, we shall always

[42] St. Augustine, *De Civitate Dei*, bk. 12, chap. 18.
[43] 1 Cor 13:12.
[44] James 1:18.
[45] Florenski, *La Colonne*, 310.
[46] Rom 8:25.

have to keep coming back to the "prophetic word" that prevents us from getting lost amidst misleading sublimities, to that little light which shows us where to set our feet on the narrow path of our earthly lives,[47] that word which emits only a shaded light "like a lamp in a dark place, until the day begins to dawn and the morning star arises in our hearts."[48] And always, in order to "enter into the fullness of God", we shall have to believe, with St. Paul, in the love of Christ "which surpasses all knowledge".[49]

Is this not what the *Divine Comedy* suggests when, just as the poet is finally about to enter the dwelling place of the divinity, Beatrice herself withdraws and St. Bernard replaces her to bring Dante through the last gateway? At that decisive instant "the Christian soul begs love to bring it

[47] "*Lucerna pedibus meis et lumen semitis meis*": Ps 119:105.

[48] 2 Pet 1:19. Cf. Maurice de la Taille, "Quelques précisions sur la révélation et le dogme", in *Etudes* 101, 513: "Vision will bear witness then to the genuineness of the acts of faith by which I anticipated it. Everything will be surpassed, nothing will be denied; and expectation will be surprised only by seeing how it has found fulfillment overabundantly."

[49] Eph 3:19. Cf. Heinrich Schlier, "La Connaissance de Dieu d'après les épîtres de saint Paul", in the anthology *Le Message de Jésus et l'interprétation moderne* (Paris: Cerf, 1969), 207–31; St. Irenaeus, *Adversus Haereses*, bk. 4, 12, 7, on 1 Cor 13 (SC vol. 100, 2, 514–15).

beyond intelligence";[50] but then, in the transfiguration of all being which is consummated in
God, love and intelligence are one.[51]

---

[50] Etienne Gilson, *La Philosophie de saint Bonaventure* (Vrin,
1924), 7.

[51] On the connection between our present knowledge of
faith, *per speculum et in aenigmate*, in the light of eternity, one
might reread with profit the letters exchanged in 1909 and
1910 in *Annales de philosophie chrétienne* between Fr. Pierre
Rousselot and Fr. Lucien Laberthonnière. M. Louis Boisset
had the excellent idea of joining these to a new edition of the
latter's articles on *Dogme et théologie* (Paris: Gembloux, 1977).
It is regrettable only that the editor does not seem to have
fully understood either the real point at issue in the discussion
or the deep sources of the two opposing points of view. Since
he is not too familiar with the period, already long past, he
too readily believes that all the theologians discussed by
Laberthonnière were men "satisfied with ready-made affirmations" and favoring a dogmatism that leaves out time
and tends to rationalism. In the case of Rousselot and that of
Lebreton, this is sheer nonsense. The editor does not seem to
have any idea that the "Copernican revolution" which he
attributes (exaggeratedly) to Vatican II's Constitution *Dei
Verbum* had already been introduced, or at least prepared for,
by Fr. Lebreton (who showed how Jesus Christ himself was
"revelation": *"mediator simul et plenitudo totius revelationis"*.
Cf. my commentary on *Dei Verbum* [Paris: Cerf, 1968],
chap. 1). Nor does he seem to realize that, among the adversaries of a rationalistic type of extrinsicism, few were more
ardent than Rousselot. Let us add that, while he unreservedly
takes sides with Laberthonnière, the editor does not seem to

Such is Christian hope. *Ex umbris et imaginibus in veritatem.*[52] "As for us", said that great Christian Charles Du Bos, "for us on whom even here below God had bestowed a light, however flickering and fragile it may be, we must spend ourselves propagating it as far as we can, and do so in the bosom of hope . . . , in the bosom of the hope that what today we see in a glass darkly, in the obscurity of faith, all of us, beyond time, may see in the full light, and face to face."[53]

Faith, charity and hope trudge on in the night. They believe the incredible; they love something

---

have understood him very well, since he comments on his works, strangely enough, by quoting authors like Paul Tillich, Charles Wackenheim, P. Hégy and G. Morel.

[52] As is well known, this was one of Newman's mottoes.

[53] Quoted by Pierre Franceschini in *Cahiers Charles du Bos* 22 (June, 1978): 62. "Historically speaking, starting with the man Jesus, a phylum of religious thinking appeared in the human mass"—and this is the Church. "If we refuse to recognize the Christian reality, we shall see the vault of the universe, which for an instant had been half-opened, closing again over our heads"; but if on the contrary we are willing "to see in the living thought of the Church the *reflection*, adapted to our state of development, of the divine thoughts, then the movement of our spirit can go forward once more": Pierre Teilhard de Chardin, *Esquisse d'une dialectique de l'ésprit* (1946), collected in *Oeuvres* (Paris: Seuil, 1963), vol. 7, 154–55; italics added.

that escapes them and leaves them behind; they hope against all hope. It is by death, i.e., by the destruction of all clearly perceptible unity, that they become one. . . . There are certain privileged hours when God allows man to perceive, either in a flash of intuition or in a moment of peaceful contemplation, vast panoramas of divine truth beheld almost from God's point of view. At such times the incomprehensible can be lighted up in a shattering instant and penetrates into the believer's field of experience. But whoever loves and believes will not demand any such *gnosis* . . . he prefers to remain in an attitude of receptive trust. . . . Whenever the understanding of his faith is offered to him he welcomes it with open arms and lets himself be led on by it to a deeper love . . . [but] a filial spirit does not try to seize what does not belong to it. It is one of the marvels of our relationship with God that maturity and the childlike spirit grow in the same degree. . . . In the eyes of reason that regulates everything in this world, the Spirit can and must seem to be anarchic chaos. Charity and faith know him and abide by him.[54]

---

[54] Hans Urs von Balthasar, *De l'intégration: aspects d'une théologie de l'histoire*, French trans. Bourboulon et al. (Brussels and Paris: DDB, 1970), 107–8.

3. ASCESIS, TRANSFORMATION, SYNTHESIS

If such is the case, it is not first of all by scrutinizing the pathways of mystery, even with sacred respect and not with that spirit of curiosity which characterizes every *gnosis*, that the Christian will enter upon the way of salvation. As we have seen, the supernatural does not merely *elevate* nature (this traditional term is correct, but it is inadequate by itself); it does not penetrate nature merely to help it prolong its momentum (the infinite does not prolong the finite) and bring it to a successful conclusion. It *transforms* it. Here again we meet this word "transformation" with its two related ideas of metamorphosis and of transfiguration, both traditional too, with solid scriptural bases, to which it is important that we give a moment's attention.

"Behold, I make all things new!" (Rev 21:5). Christianity is "a doctrine of transformation"[55] because the Spirit of Christ comes to permeate the first creation and make of it a "new creature".

---

[55] Tresmontant, *La Mystique chrétienne*, 187. In this section we shall borrow several passages from this work, and shall follow the direction indicated in its fourth chapter: "La Mort et la signification de l'ascèse". See also idem, *La Crise moderniste* (Paris: Seuil, 1979), chap. 10.

What is true of the final great transformation, on the occasion of the "Parousia" at which there will arise "new heavens and a new earth" (Rev 21), is already true now, according to St. Paul, of each one of us. "We await the Savior, our Lord Jesus Christ, who will refashion the body of our lowness, making it like unto the body of his glory" (Phil 3:20–21). But we need to be changed already, in the depths of our being, "transformed into his image" (2 Cor 3:18). So St. Paul exhorts us to allow ourselves to be "transformed in the renewal of our minds" (Rom 12:2).[56] This is very different from a simple continuation. For each of us, as for the universe, this means undergoing death in view of a rebirth. In a letter to his friend Werhlé, Blondel criticized "that simple-minded optimism of some neo-Christians who would like to see in the supernatural life nothing more than the full flowering of our dearest aspirations. Divine love is something altogether different from this insipid harmony."[57] Claude Tresmontant cites many passages from St. Teresa and St. John of the Cross which recall in vigorous language the link between "transformation" and "union", or, as

[56] The three words are: μετασχηματίσει, μεταμορφούμεθα, μεταμορφοῦσθε.

[57] Maurice Blondel and Johannès Wehrlé, *Correspondance*, ed. Henri de Lubac (Paris: Aubier-Montaigne, 1969), vol. 1, 349.

the latter saint says in a compact formula, "trans-formation into God" (prologue of the *Living Flame of Love*). Such is the principle of *Christian asceticism*; it is not contempt for the body or for any gift of the first creation, nor some sort of training imposed on our human nature to enable it to perform certain feats in its own order; it is the indispensable condition for realization of the union of these two incommensurables: God and man.

This is something that Blondel stressed over and over, especially in his correspondence with his friend Fr. Laberthonnière, copiously quoted by Claude Tresmontant. Here are some passages:

> God being what he is, the supernatural elevation of man is conceivable, is possible only through an operation which is totally different from simple expansion or the simple moral communication of wills. . . . We must not imagine that man can make the journey to God with ease. . . . We must keep in mind the *natural* heterogeneity distin-guishing God and man. . . . There is an abyss that must be bridged. . . . Divine love has found the way to *communicate what is incommunicable* . . . [but] God cannot fail to be himself. And to make us his, to make us over into himself, there is a trial, a transformation in love that must be suffered and willed, so that this incommunicable

One may communicate himself without ceasing to be himself and without our ceasing to be ourselves. . . . The Gospel, however fully human it may be, still shows this specific characteristic: that it demands a *denuo nasci*. . . . We must then resolve either to take this "revelation" seriously or else to remain in the domain of an a-Christian wisdom; and I call by that name the wisdom which would see in Christ nothing but a moral paradigm . . . valuable because of his example, not by his action which is intimate and *transforming* and deifies us in the strict sense.[58]

Such was St. Paul's teaching and that of the great Christian mystics. This doctrine is somewhat neglected and even at times compromised by the over-rationalistic systematizations of theolo-

[58] Maurice Blondel and Lucien Laberthonnière, *Correspondance philosophique* (Paris: Seuil, 1962), for the years 1921, 1923 and 1925. Quoted by Tresmontant in *La Mystique chrétienne*; other quotations, 138–41. "There must be separation", comments Tresmontant, 145; but "the worst evil of all would be to settle down in the land of Egypt, to grow satisfied with the provisory and ephemeral, to attach oneself to an order of things that is already out-of-date." And on 160: "Ascesis is a universal condition for the birth of the new man, for the transformation needed so that man may attain the full stature planned for him by the Creator. . . . Below this ascesis, below that . . . metamorphosis which requires an ascesis, there is found only a larval, puerile state. . . ."

gians. Blondel knew how to take up again and
give it new strength, and it is this same teaching
that Fr. Teilhard de Chardin tried to express by
his reiterated use of the words "transformation",
"metamorphosis" and "transfiguration".[59] Each
of us, in proportion to our measure of grace and
our state, must accept this doctrine.

On the other hand, since in Jesus Christ the
Transcendent made itself (partially) immanent,
since God's gift has been implanted in the depths
of man's nature—for the two elements which we
deal with here, nature and the supernatural, have
not become an intermixture or confusion but have
been joined in intimate union in dependence on
and in the image of the two natures in Christ[60]—
it would be useless and not in conformity with
Christian reality constantly to seek in the com-
plexity of concrete situations and tasks a "specific
Christian note" which would need to be cultivated
by itself, jealously preserving it against all con-

[59] Blondel and Teilhard, *Correspondance*, passim; Henri de
Lubac, *La Pensée religieuse du Père Teilhard de Chardin* (Paris:
Aubier-Montaigne, 1962), chap. 11, "Nature et grâce" and
chap. 12, "Transfiguration du cosmos".

[60] The "boundary line" established at Chalcedon, which
keeps the two natures distinct and not compounded, "is not
really a boundary line; in fact it is there to make possible the
immediate union, the holy espousals between God and the
creature": Von Balthasar, *La Foi du Christ*, 79.

tamination with the human, and keeping it in its supposed "purity". Such separatism, if carried to the extreme, would be doubly fatal. The supernatural, as we have shown and as we must keep repeating, is not a "supernature" with its own consistency and its own subsistence, something which would be superadded to human nature, to all its developments and to all that it creates (to all its acquired culture). Nor does it eliminate that nature. It neither disdains nor replaces it. It informs it, remolds it; if necessary it can exorcise it (we shall see more of this further on); it transfigures it in all of its concepts and activities. As has been said with reference to St. John of the Cross, "the supernatural permeates and spiritualizes the natural order, without, for all that, depriving it of its rights and its riches."[61] The Word of God on coming into this world did not try to compete on the same level, as if he had been only one more element in this world, with all that humanity could offer, all that was true, just, beautiful, upright and praiseworthy in individual behavior or in the social life of men.[62] He did not come like a ravaging power, devastating in his conquest men's spontaneous religious sense or all the ac-

[61] Alex Ceslas Rzewuski, *A travers l'invisible cristal: confessions d'un dominicain* (Ploy, 1976), 384.
[62] Cf. Phil 4:8.

quisitions of their moral culture; he came demanding total renewal. St. Augustine was faithful to his spirit when he explained in the *City of God* that the Roman virtues and the natural principle of virtue were awaiting their purification and their completion from the "true religion".[63] We cannot, therefore (if we may be allowed to speak very schematically), reject "religion" as something merely human and give its place to "faith" alone as something received from God; nor can we disparage "morality" while exalting a more or less eschatological hope, nor neglect whatever can be included in the four "cardinal" virtues to exalt a pure "charity" lacking all roots and any natural environment. The greatest spiritual writers in the Christian tradition: St. Gregory, St. Bernard, etc., showed on the contrary the greatest interest in this quadruple basis: prudence, justice, fortitude and temperance;[64] St. Thomas gave them considerable space in his *Summa Theologica*,[65] and did not for that reason deserve the name of syncretist or

[63] St. Augustine, *De Civitate Dei*, bk. 2, chap. 29; cf. bk. 15, chap. 12, 16 and 17. We know, too, all that the humanism of the Middle Ages and that of the Christian Renaissance owe to the fifth book of *De Doctrina Christiana*.

[64] St. Bernard, *De Consideratione*, bk. 1, chap. 8, in *Opera*, ed. Jean Leclercq (Rome, 1957), vol. 2, etc.

[65] Cf. *Summa Theologica* II–II.

naturalist that some have wanted to give him. If the three theological virtues of faith, hope and charity do not carry out with their divine power their mission of informing, purifying, deepening and bringing to their fulfillment man's authentic human values, it is much to be feared that they themselves will be impoverished, will wither away and become denatured.[66]

There is no doubt about it whatsoever; in no individual, no given social structure, no century, has the Christian synthesis ever been fully realized, nor will it ever be. Perfect harmony can never be achieved. What might be mistaken for a marvellous degree of equilibrium would probably be the start of a corruption. Thus (to take but one example, clear enough in its general terms), a perfect Christian civilization, or even a rather imperfect one, has never existed in history and never will. And when we look upon societies which, although rejecting Christ for all practical

[66] Whence, in the Constitution *Gaudium et spes*, the discussion of "man's vocation", which is at once the Christian vocation of man and the human vocation of the Christian. With Pierre Colin we should note that "the two ideas of creation and of vocation to communion with God are always connected. The Council never speaks of man as a creature of God without reminding him that his Creator calls him to be united in Christ with the divinity": "Le Concile et le sens de l'homme", in *Recherches et débats* 57:143, 148–49.

purposes, have preserved only an empty appearance or a deformed choice of Christian principles and virtues and still hypocritically call themselves Christian, we can understand how Maurice Clavel, with his customary acerbity, says that such "Christian" civilization gives him nausea.[67] It is still true that the historian can note in society many achievements due to the influence of Christianity, for example the changes in Roman law which followed the conversion of Constantine, the patient education of a still barbarous Europe, the many institutions created during the Middle Ages to further the cause of peace and protect the weak against secular power, the widespread reaction against the brutality of morals. A number of serious and impartial historians have established these facts, today often forgotten or misrepresented by an atmosphere of resentment against the past history of the Church. Of course there were two sides to many of these facts, and the accomplishments remained cruelly imperfect. It is well to stress this so as not to arouse puerile hopes; no particular civilization will ever fully deserve the name "Christian", far from it. The notion of Christian civilization does not represent either a past which some would like to see brought back, or a future on

[67] M. Clavel, *Deux siècles chez Lucifer* (Paris: Seuil, 1977), 288.

whose arrival one can count. It is an outline, an ideal, not a blueprint drawn up in advance, but a definite orientation. We might say if we like, in words that are accepted today, that it is a myth; but a myth which a Christian, even one who is on his guard against all idealistic dreams, can never entirely give up pursuing. "The Christian transfiguration of the universe within time is a myth. But it is still our duty to tend towards it, and it is by doing so that partial achievements come about; and these are not myths. Furthermore, thanks to this myth, known for what it is, these partial successes will never be taken for the attainment of perfection."[68]

On the other hand, experience as well as reflection show that by preventing man from halting and basking at a certain point of equilibrium, individual or social, but still simply human, the infusion of the supernatural instills into him the principle of a fresh disequilibrium that confers

[68] Yves de Montcheuil, *Le Royaume et ses exigences* (Editions de l'Epi, 1957), 91. By the same author, see also "L'Idée de la civilisation chrétienne", in *L'Eglise et le monde actuel*, 2nd ed. (Editions du Témoignage chrétien et de l'Epi, 1945), 23–24. This work as a whole constitutes a commentary made in advance of the principles that underlie the Constitution *Gaudium et spes*. The author was not naive enough to imagine that any given civilization, present or future, could ever fully deserve the title "Christian".

on him a superior type of nobility but that also leads to his torment. And if human wisdom is a pinnacle, holiness (to come back to Pascal's saying) is something belonging to "a different order". Still, throughout the ever changing circumstances which force man perpetually to invent new things and to battle without ceasing, equilibrium, harmony and synthesis remain something to be sought.[69]

[69] On this point see the reflections of Gérard Soulages in "Le Christianisme et l'Europe", a lecture given at Brussels on October 27, 1979, for the eleventh Congress of the Association of St. Benedict, Patron of Europe: "The four cardinal virtues: prudence, courage, temperance and justice, elevate all man's powers, those of his intellect, his will and his affective life, balancing them with each other and thus adapting man to himself and to others. They are above all the result of education; and they reveal to us an admirable type of humanity, something like a Greek temple, where everything is measured, ordered, balanced and in harmony. But the paradox is that in the midst of this measured order, this harmonious equilibrium, Christianity introduces a sort of exaggeration, and in a sense an element of disorder, an unexpected lack of balance, a higher folly which dislocates and renews everything. This superior folly, these amazing calls to exaggeration, are called faith, hope and charity. We cannot doubt it: the theological virtues are fed by a terrible fire, the fire of the living God himself, and this fire burns our souls with a mortal burn, the burn of the infinite. 'Be perfect as your heavenly Father is perfect. . . . Sell all you have, and come, follow me!'

At one time a violent campaign was launched, without any serious discernment, against the very idea of "Christian culture" or "Christian humanism", as well as against every notion of "the sacred" or of "religion"—all this in the name of "pure faith" or "secular faith". Still, it is not very difficult to understand that unless it is a pseudoculture, all formalism and superficiality, no culture is really neutral. The culture of a Christian must also be Christian unless he is prepared to betray his faith or at least to let it vegetate without any assimilative force. This does not mean that such a culture will be nourished only by spe-

---

"Between the man molded by the Greek virtues and the man renewed by the fire of faith, there must be an abyss. The folly of the Cross can with difficulty join hands with the wisdom of the ancients. But if for an individual a certain dislocation of his humanity by the jealous love of the living God is in the long run a priceless grace, from the point of view of society and of civilization one might fear that such dislocations would lead to catastrophes. But this has not occurred. The Christian absolute never bewitched the human conscience; it enriched it in depth and consolidated it most remarkably. Medieval man is a being capable of tenderness and pity, renewed by charity. He is a metaphysical spirit, far stronger than the man of antiquity who was tempted by scepticism or by the illuminism of *gnosis*. . . . He bears within himself an infinite longing for truth and the taste for rationality. Henceforth such a man is armed; he can go forth to the conquest of the universe."

cifically Christian elements: quite the contrary. It will be all the deeper and all the more Christian the more human elements it draws on, borrowed from the most varied sources; but all of them must be enlightened, judged, criticized, transformed and unified by this assimilating principle called faith that is nourished by them. We might say much the same thing about Christian humanism. That name can also cover some very different realities. Maurice Clavel wrote: "If humanism is the doctrine of the absolute existence of man, of man alone, to the exclusion of God, then I am anti-humanist." This every Christian must obviously approve; but he went on to say: "If humanism is the doctrine of the absolute value of man, then I am a humanist", and this time too we could not have put it better ourselves.[70] There exists, no doubt, more as a state of mind than as a doctrine, a certain "Christian humanism" in which Christianity appears as something secondary in practice, the main concern being reserved for the purely human elements that a faith which has remained remote and imprecise timidly comes to crown. But there is another type of Christian humanism which on the contrary is fully in conformity with the logic of faith, trusting in its

[70] M. Clavel, *Dieu est Dieu* (Grasset, 1976), 170.

assimilative force.[71] More than one genuine saint can be found among its representatives.

More and more, however, the term "humanism" is used to indicate a doctrine or at least an attitude which deliberately stops short at man, neglecting or even disregarding altogether any anterior and superior being, refusing to recognize in man "every desire which would provide his will with an infinite exigency", and would furnish him with "the indispensable potential of energy" needed to satisfy it.[72] "My deepest conviction", said Renan long ago in that unctuous and equivocal language which had so quickly become his trademark, "is that the religion of the future will be pure *humanism*, i.e., the cult of whatever is from man, all of life sanctified and uplifted to a moral value. Then the law and the prophets will be: 'Take care of your lovely humanity.' "[73] And Simone de Beauvoir, with her imperious tendency to impose her own definition and her set prejudice of considering the

[71] Cf. some efforts at clarification in my study of *Pic de la Mirandole* (Paris: Aubier-Montaigne, 1974), pt. 2, chap. 1: "Religion et humanisme".

[72] Cf. Claude Bruaire, *L'Affirmation de Dieu: essai sur la logique de l'existence* (Paris: Seuil, 1964), 39.

[73] E. Renan, *L'Avenir de la science*, 2nd ed. (1890), 101. The words in italics are, he says, "an admirable expression borrowed from Schiller".

God of Christians as a "foreigner": "What defines
all humanism is that the moral world is not a
world which is imposed, something alien to man
and to which he must try to find entrance from
without. No, it is a world willed by man himself."[74]
Clearly, such a humanism cannot be Christianized;
but it is no less clear to us that the man which it
seeks to exalt is a rootless being; "cut off from
nature and lacking any contact with real transcendence, he condemns himself to solipsism."[75]
His fruitless efforts at "autotranscendence" do not
provide him with a refuge against the slaveries
that threaten him. It has been said of this sort
of "exclusive humanism" that it resembles a cut
flower, and that nobody knows "how long it will
last".[76] In fact, its duration already seems seriously
compromised; and among its heirs there is com-
petition as to who will proclaim himself, in
one sense or another, the most resolutely "anti-
humanist". Christian humanism has more future.

The *a priori* rejection of "religion" and of the

---

[74] Simone de Beauvoir, *Pour une morale de l'ambiguité* (Paris:
Gallimard, 1947), 199. The Christian can only refuse such a
dichotomy: "*Deus, interior intime meo et superior summo meo*"
(St. Augustine).

[75] Bruaire, *L'Affirmation de Dieu*.

[76] Golo Mann, quoted by Auer in *Ich glaube* (French trans.
Je crois [Namur and Paris: Lethielleux, 1978], 152).

"sacred" arises from a misunderstanding similar to that which led to the refusal to accept the idea of a Christian culture.[77] Not only was this an insult to man, it was also a corruption of the Gospel. The partisans of this theory have often invoked the double patronage of Karl Barth and of Dietrich Bonhoeffer. But the influence of these two theologians, like that of a certain trend in Protestantism which seems to delight in antitheses, is far from explaining everything. Neither Bonhoeffer (in spite of some passages in his letters from prison, inspired by the circumstances, when he might well have believed in the hegemony established by Nazism) nor Barth, who was reacting against a liberal Protestantism's religiosity which lacked any depth of faith, really professed such simplistic views.[78] It is clear that the notion of religion

[77] Cf. de Lubac, *La Foi chrétienne*, chap. 4: "Foi, croyance, religion".

[78] See the moderate criticism of the positions of Barth and Bonhoeffer in Gustave Thils, *Christianisme sans religion?* (Casterman, 1968), pt. 3. It was in virtue of another similar misunderstanding that the expansion of the monastic life has often been seen as a phenomenon that was not Christian. (One might as well say that the liturgy is not a Christian phenomenon.) No doubt, of course, as Antoine Guillaumont reminds us, "there is a 'constant' in the monastic phenomenon which can be observed equally well in the Indian

is an analogical one; a phenomenology with any
pretention to exact thinking cannot apply it uni-
vocally to what are called the "primitive" religions,
to the religions of vast empires or great civilizations,
or to "universal" religions. Many historians would
hesitate to include Buddhism in the general category of religion; because of other characteristic
traits the hesitation would be even greater as regards Christianity. Even from the merely historical
point of view Christianity is in a class by itself; but
it is precisely this fact (something that the believer
grasps) which enables it to embrace fully, not the
other religions in a sort of higher syncretism, but
religion in its human essence. As early as the first
volume of his *Church Dogmatics*, Barth himself did

Brahman monasticism and in that of Buddhism" ("La Conception du désert chez les moines d'Egypte", in *Revue de
l'histoire des religions* 188, 1 [July, 1975]: 17). "For a phenomenology of monasticism", the historian must show this
constant and must seek out the facts and the elements that lie
at *the origin of Christian monasticism* (the words in italics are the
title of a book by Antoine Guillaumont [Bellefontaine,
1979]). But the monastic life in the Church is a Christianized
religious movement, and so deeply Christianized from the
very beginning in its principal motivation and in its spirit that
one must admit that it is fully Christian (notwithstanding, of
course, the many human deficiencies found in its historical
realizations).

not fear to affirm that "the Christian religion is the true religion."[79] And Pastor Visser't Hooft is his faithful interpreter when he writes in his memoirs: "At the beginning of 1924 I tried for the first time to slip what I had learned from Barth into a talk on 'faith and religion'. I tried to explain the radical difference between a religiosity centered on man and a faith centered on God."[80]

In view of the ravages caused by the above-mentioned campaign (sometimes efforts were made, against all evidence, to base it on the Council!), a certain retreat has taken place during these recent years; but this has only led to more internal disequilibrium, a no less fatal dislocation. The same lack of consistency in thought has immediately driven the same people to the opposite extreme. Unashamedly, they have celebrated the "return of the sacred"; a "powerful counterattack by religion" in a "syncretistic context".[81] With

[79] Karl Barth, *Dogmatique*, trans. Ryser (Geneva, 1972), vol. 1, chap. 2, 115; cf. 133.

[80] Visser't Hooft, *Le Temps du rassemblement* (Paris: Seuil, 1975), 28. The author modestly adds: "But as I had not fully assimilated Barth's theology, I do not believe that my audience of students understood very well what I was trying to say."

[81] J. P. Torrell, O.P., *Revue thomiste* (1979), 281.

no regard for genuine Christianity, today every species of the "sacred" or even every tawdry imitation thereof,[82] every religion, every spirituality, every culture is being exalted, amid total confusion and with no effort at discrimination. Here and there clerics, who despite their name had been asleep in profoundest ignorance, are dazzled by the discovery of the vast universe; they are quite prepared to admire everything about it without understanding it and have no critical resources (or what they believe to be such) except against the faith which nourished them. They have become blind to the unique contribution of Judeo-Christian revelation, as well as to the lights, overpowering or discreet, shed by holiness.

[82] Regarding the "category of the sacred", see below, Appendix E; and Henri Bouillard, *Le Sacré: études et recherches* (Paris: Aubier-Montaigne, 1974), 33–56. On the "ambiguities and the articulations of the sacred", see Antoine Vergote, "L'Esprit, puissance de salut et de santé spirituelle", in *Expérience de l'Esprit: mélanges Schillebeeckx*, eds. Paul Brand et al. (Paris: Beauchesne, 1976), 411–29. On the topic treated in this whole section one should reread Péguy. See also Cardinal Wojtyla, *Le Signe de contradiction*, a retreat given at the Vatican, trans. Thérèse Wilkanowicz (Paris: Fayard, 1979), 196–97.

4. TRANSCENDENCE

As we have suggested above, in the temporal existence of an individual no less than in the entire history of humanity, even putting things at their best in a sort of idealistic dream, the synthesis cannot be fully achieved, not only *de facto*, but even *de jure*. For the supernatural end of man, his only end, is "eternal life" (Jn 6:27; Rom 5:21, etc.), which is poured out by the Holy Spirit into the depths of the human heart but cannot flower fully save in circumstances wholly other than those of space and time. The Christian must be on his guard not to fall into the delusion of a "supernaturalism" which would either make him neglect his truly human tasks, i.e., in the terms of our distinction his "natural" tasks; or, on the contrary, allow him to become so absorbed by them as to take them for his ultimate end—and by that very fact accomplish them badly. In the order of knowledge, esthetics or action, such a delusion would be fatal.[83] It would mean taking as eternal what Fr. Teilhard de Chardin did not hesitate to call, from the point of view of the absolute, "the tawdry

[83] Cf. Jules Monchanin, *De l'esthétique à la mystique*, 2nd ed. (Casterman, 1967).

outer husk of every figure". "To the various human constructions", he also said, "I attribute no definitive or absolute value; I believe that they will disappear, compounded into something new and unimaginable."[84] There is, in fact, an "entropy" of culture just as there is one found in inanimate nature; and since the world as a whole is going to its death, "it cannot be considered as an immanent reflection or an anticipation of the Kingdom of God". Hence it cannot be, as such, the goal of our hopes.

We must, then, take care not to confuse the "progress of this world" (itself a very ambivalent term) with the "new creation". We must avoid slipping from conversion of heart, by which the "new man" is born in Christ, to the unfolding of history (dialectic or not) that bears "as in its womb" the societies of the future.[85] We shall not fail to distinguish as very different things the pursuit of a good social organization, or the deter-

[84] Letters to Fr. Auguste Valensin, December 8 and 12, 1919. This, of course, did not prevent him from valuing highly the indispensable role played by the "figure" and its progress in temporal existence. See Blondel and Teilhard, *Correspondance*, 27 and 63.

[85] As some seem to have tried to do, thinking that they were prolonging the work of Fr. Fessard; *France catholique* (Nov. 16, 1979), 11. See below, chapter 3, part 1.

mination of a more successful policy, and the beginning of the Kingdom of God; they are two different orders of reality. The first of these is not to be rejected; it is certainly worthy of active interest and even of passionate dedication which can become obligatory in certain cases, even apart from all ideology. Further, no matter how fundamental and how strict such a distinction may be, it must not be understood as a separation. The two pursuits are in a reciprocal relation. Let us say, quoting the words of Paul VI,[86] that "there are deep and close ties between evangelization and human progress, development, liberation." It may be a difficult task, but it is one that no theology of history can turn its back on in our day: to establish "a positive relationship between the progress of the modern world and the coming of the Kingdom." A wholly disinterested seeking for the Kingdom in the depths of men's hearts can have considerable consequences, in ways that no one can foresee, on the emergence of a better society; and on the other hand it can be legitimate, without pursuing utopias, to seek in such a society some sort of "parable", some distant foreshadowing of

[86] *Evangelii nuntiandi*, no. 31. Cf. Achiel Peelman, *La Théologie de l'histoire de Balthasar* (Berne, 1978), 50.

the Kingdom.[87] How could one refuse to join in the ardent prayer that Péguy, in his *Mystère de la charité*, puts on Joan of Arc's lips:

> May all this earth be like a heaven on earth;
> May all men's hearts beat as one. . . ,
> May the earth be a beginning of heaven,
>   a beginning of heaven. . . .[88]

Still, we must make no mistake about it, and here the insistence is not superfluous: "All man's works, and among them his most ambitious achievement, civilization, are necessarily condemned to failure; there is no perfect success found within his earthly history."[89] And so many of his successes bear within themselves the seeds of their opposites! Furthermore, we must not promise ourselves "what the Gospel does not promise. . . . Our holy Scriptures foretell for us, in our times, nothing but trials, torments, evils and

---

[87] Cf. Etienne Gilson, *Les Metamorphoses de la cité de Dieu* (Louvain: Publications universitaires de Louvain, 1952), 291: "The city of men cannot arise in the shadow of the Cross save as a suburb of the city of God."

[88] Péguy, "Le Mystère de la charité de Jeanne d'Arc", in *Oeuvres en prose, 1898–1914*, vol. 2, 1403.

[89] Henri Marrou, *Théologie de l'histoire* (Paris: Seuil, 1968), 173. Cf. Henri de Lubac, *Paradoxes, suivis de nouveaux paradoxes*, new ed. (Paris: Seuil, 1959).

temptations."[90] Above all we need to remember that all human achievements are mortal and that in their short existence they always remain ambivalent. Mortal indeed: the secular theology of Robinson or Cox, which recently enjoyed a rather contrived popularity, "has no theology of death. It is all very well to say, as both of them do insistently, that a Christian should not spend his time in this world as if he really lived somewhere else. But it is very erroneous to give the impression, as both authors seem to do, that the Christian should live in this world as if he would always remain in it."[91] Ambivalent, also: the best social organization (supposing that such an abstraction really means anything, or that it could possibly be brought about concretely even for a single fugitive instant) might be just as capable of leading men away from the Kingdom. When Jesus asks whether the Son of Man on his return will find faith on earth, he does not say that society will not be, in men's opinion, in a state of advanced civilization. People have very rightly spoken of the "Gospel revolution", and it is true that that

[90] St. Augustine, *In Psalm.* 39, 28; quoted by Marrou, *Théologie de l'histoire*, 185.

[91] Robert L. Richard, *Secularization Theology*, 169; quoted by E. L. Mascall, *Théologie de l'avenir*, French trans. Delteil (Desclée, 1970), 84–85.

revolution, precisely because it goes infinitely deeper than any other, is still far from having borne all its fruits, far from having reached its fullest dimensions. But the "Gospel revolutionaries" are not utopians; they refuse to be imprisoned

in the impossible contradiction of an absolute which would come to pass here below. . . . They do not make idols of themselves, or of the world or time or history. . . . They know, of course, that the temporal bears the eternal within it. . . . But they also know that the two do not coincide and that the first creation must go through the fire of death before it can come to life again in the second creation, for there is nothing belonging to man which will escape destruction. Like man himself, the human city must die in order to live again. . . .[92]

To reiterate this same basic idea in the words which must be used today, let us say that one must no longer mistake what has been called, often in a confused way, man's "liberation" or his

[92] Jean Bastaire, "Le Socialisme à l'épreuve de la foi", *Feuillets de l'amitié Charles Péguy* 214 (Jan.–March, 1977): 14–15. "To change its way of living means not only uprooting its structures, its customs, its institutions, but questioning its ontological status. . . ." Cf. my study on "La Recherche d'un homme nouveau", in *Affrontements mystiques* (Paris: Témoignage chrétien, 1949), esp. 88–92.

"advancement" (social or intellectual) with his salvation.[93] The former of these two aims (understood as a social concern and not as a myth) can take on, and in many specific cases *does* take on, a character of urgency; and the disciples of the Gospel should be among the first to consecrate their efforts to it. But it remains a human concern—and hence how could one forget that in all this effort men put forth there lies great danger, either of seeking false liberation, or of paving the way to a greater injustice, or of arriving at a result just the opposite of what one had sought? Does history not show us startling instances of this? How could one fail to see that "repression today presents itself under the admirable aspects of liberation"?[94] Salvation is a gift of God; it is entry into the Kingdom, the Kingdom preached by Jesus, which cannot be "won by political struggles, nor grasped by men's speculations", nor even conquered by their moral efforts. "One cannot", whether for oneself or for the world, "plan for it, organize it, build it,

[93] As we mentioned above, when Paul VI indicated their relationship, he at the same time distinguished them from each other.

[94] Edgar Morin, *Le Paradigme perdu: la nature humaine* (Paris: Seuil, 1974), 208: "Its wiles are almost invincible, at least so long as it has not taken over power; when it does, it crushes all opposition. . . ."

construct it"; one cannot even "imagine it or get any idea of it; for it is something given, a bequest; we can only inherit it. The coming of God's Kingdom is a miracle and action of God."[95] In its social meaning liberation of every kind belongs to time; salvation is for eternity, and for that reason always anticipates time. We should not even say, strictly speaking, that the more or less perfect accomplishment (it always remains imperfect) of the first of these two goals is at least the indispensable preparation for the second; for this would amount to saying that Christian hope is necessarily situated in the prolongation of the objective results obtained by human efforts. It can and must blos-

---

[95] W. Kasper, *Jésus le Christ*, trans. J. Désignaux and A. Liefooghe (Paris: Cerf, 1976), 116–17; Mt 21:43; Lk 12:32; 22:29. "We would not be faithful to the Gospel if we did not believe that the Kingdom of heaven begins here below": Alfred Ancel, *Dialogue en vérité* (Editions sociales, 1979). But we would certainly be unfaithful to it if we gave the impression that its beginning would coincide here below with the advent of "a socialist society" (or indeed of any particular society at all). The mistake made by a Christian cannot consist in "deferring the establishment of such a society until after Christ's return"; it would consist in linking the "Kingdom", before or after that return, to such an establishment. "The Kingdom of God comes unseen by men's eyes; there will be no saying: See, it is here! or: See, it is there! The Kingdom of God is here, within you" (Lk 17:20–21).

som also in the most desperate as well as in the most promising human circumstances. This is not, need we repeat, to deny or to neglect the obligation of promoting true human "liberation" as far as one can—without paying too much attention to the "wise and prudent ones" of this world, no matter how well intentioned. And one will feel himself all the more inclined to work for this goal in proportion as one does not allow himself to be beguiled by quixotic hopes. Faced with such a task, every Christian must keep in mind the words of St. Paul: "The charity of Christ urges us on."[96]

In his posthumous little book, a collection of spiritual instructions on *Le Royaume et ses exigences*, Fr. Yves de Montcheuil, who had devoted a considerable portion of his theological work to establishing the relationships between nature and the supernatural as we have tried to set them forth here, and who, as is well known, was deeply and heroically involved in his times, used energetic language to stress the absolute transcendence of God's Kingdom as Jesus proclaimed it, beyond all temporal purposes which today are summed up for us (so imperfectly) in the three terms: justice, liberation and social advancement.

---

[96] Cf. Yves de Montcheuil, *L'Eglise et le monde actuel*, 127–37: "Activité chrétienne et activité temporelle".

Entry into the Kingdom is a new birth. It is the source of a life which is superior to a well-organized natural life, a life which belongs to a different, supernatural order. It is the principle of a prayer which has no other end but itself, which corresponds with the soul's need to be present to God even as God is present to it. The Kingdom which has Christ as its King establishes us in a special kind of existence, beyond our natural existence. When one has understood this, one can see that the spiritual life is irreducible to the social life; that it is impossible to utilize religion as a means for establishing justice among men. To justify and to promote religion as an instrument of social progress is to allow what religion is in itself to escape. To confound the coming of the Kingdom with the advent of a better social order is to misunderstand totally the originality and value of the Kingdom.[97]

5. THE ROLE OF THE CHURCH

A correct idea of the distinction between nature and the supernatural and of their unity is also necessary for an understanding of the Church and her role. This is the direct consequence of what was said in the preceding section. Every notion which tends to bring down the supernatural order

[97] Idem, *Le Royaume*, 85–86.

to the level of nature tends, by that very fact, to mistake the Church for the world, to conceive of her after the model of human societies, to expect her to change even in her essential structures and her faith in order to suit the world's changes—and this is indeed what is taking place among a number of our contemporaries. In the past a theocratic temptation may have threatened; today, on the contrary (but because of a similar confusion, and with less excuse, given the historical context), the secularist temptation has come to the fore very strongly. Because the tendency of the times leads (to some extent) towards liberalism, some would like a representative, liberal and constitutional papacy; and because at the same time our society is evolving in a collectivist direction they tend to understand the collegial character of the Church in the form of a collective type of government.[98] These people overlook the divine laws of the Church because they no longer understand her divine mission. The Church of Christ's primary, essential, irreplaceable mission is to remind us constantly, *opportune*, *importune*, of our divine supernatural vocation and to communicate to us through her sacred ministry the seed, still fragile

[98] That is a contradiction in terms which nothing in the texts justifies and which was on many occasions rejected in advance during the meetings of the Council.

and hidden, yet real and living, of our divine life.[99] This seed must not remain sterile. The revelation of our divine vocation, along with all that flows from it, ordinarily produces its first results not only in the depths of people's hearts but likewise on the outside, in the affairs of time and of history. But in this area the supernatural impulse will afford good results only if it couples itself with all the resources of human knowledge, experience and wisdom; and experience has shown us often enough that it is very often choked, or at least slowed down, by the contrary forces. On the other hand, the role of the Church, especially in the person of her ministers, cannot be reduced to such a task; however urgent this may appear in certain cases it is never anything more than a secondary end—even when in the temporal order it may have to be put first, here or there, so as to open up a path to the Gospel. Otherwise the Church would be unfaithful to Christ, who did not preach the Kingdom of God "in order to provoke a general liberation of his people and to vanquish the Romans once for all."[100] She would

[99] 1 Jn 3:2: "οὔπω ἐφανερώθη τί ἐσόμεθα"; "*Nondum apparuit quid erimus*".

[100] Georges Hourdin, *Pour le concile* (Stock, 1977), 122. One might read the whole page (and many others) if one wished to find examples of the misunderstandings (to say

succumb to that "temporal heresy" which as Péguy observed (Péguy, who understood so well the value of the temporal) consists in proposing that the temporal should end up by "absorbing the eternal".[101] Thus losing her own soul, she would be reduced to a mere human organization, and a totally ineffective one at that. She would only be a parasite, duplicating or trying to duplicate— without having either the qualified personnel or the necessary means—the institutions that men can freely create for themselves. At that stage, she should simply disappear. And this is precisely what those whose minds are totally closed against the supernatural have been demanding for a long time. This is also—what a paradox!—just what in practice some of her misguided children are clamoring for today, when they talk about wanting a "new Church". A Church secularized, natural-ized, which would willingly give up her "cult" and replace it with "culture", seeking her "lights", not in the Gospels (even if lip service were still paid to them), but in the world; a Church which would pretend to be born today from some kind

---

nothing more) into which Christians, whose early inspiration was undoubtedly upright and generous, have allowed them-selves to be drawn. By the same author: *Dieu en liberté* (Stock, 1973).

[101] Péguy, "L'Argent suite", *Oeuvres en prose*, vol. 2, 1291.

of radical "mutation", which would no longer
concern herself, even with disinterested zeal, with
anything but the organization of life on this earth—
such a Church would have no right to exist anymore in the society of men, and would not be long
in meeting dissolution.

This shows us what sort of welcome we should
offer to the various "theologies" which present
themselves to us in these days as theologies of
"liberation", or of "development", or again as
"political theologies". It also indicates the kind of
criticism to which such ideas must be subjected.
They may be (they are not necessarily so) perfectly
orthodox, correct and opportune. Their only
drawback, but it is a fundamental one, is that they
pretend to take the place of theology itself. Even
if they aimed at something less than this, by
claiming to be self-sufficient in their limited areas,
they would still lack the only basis which would
give them a right to the name "theologies". Then,
to what ideologies would they not be handed
over?[102] This is something that the Church, which

---

[102] An example of doctrinal restatement of the question
and of clear-sightedness in this matter was given by the
posthumous book by Fr. Gaston Fessard (d. 1978), *Chrétiens
marxistes et théologie de la libération: itinéraire du Père J. Girardi*,
Le Sycomore (Paris: Lethielleux, 1978). Cf. idem, *Eglise de
France, prends garde de perdre la foi!* (Julliard, 1979). See the long

preserves the "word of salvation" and whose mission it is to transmit this word to all, cannot allow us to forget. By doing so she serves, in addition, even the temporal ends which these incomplete theologies sought to safeguard. Certainly she needs courage for this task, for on every side she encounters misunderstandings that keep springing up. But we know that amidst the vicissitudes of history, and in spite of the individual failings which always remain possible, she will not lack this essential courage. Her spiritual leaders will always be able to count on the backing of the humble and simple among the faithful who spontaneously discern, under the action of the Spirit of God, those things in the Church which are at the service of the Gospel, and those things which would empty it of meaning and smother it under other interests.

Let us therefore make it clear, in the words of Fr. Hans Urs von Balthasar:

> Criticism of the theology of liberation does not question the urgency of the practical concern which inspires it. But the totality of divine revelation in the world cannot in any case be restricted to a

---

article devoted to these two books by Michel Sales, "Praxis marxiste et discernement chrétien", in *Plamia* (*Meudon*) 53 (Christmas, 1979): 31–60.

political and social liberation, nor even to the
general concept of liberty. Theology of liberation
has its specific place within a theology of the
Kingdom of God. It offers *one* aspect of theology
as a whole, and in practice it calls on the Church to
strive to reform the world, in all its dimensions, in
conformity with Christ.[103]

[103] Hans Urs von Balthasar, "Considérations sur l'histoire
du salut, à propos de la théologie de la libération", in *Nouvelle
Revue théologique* 99 (July–Aug., 1977): 52–53. See also the
declaration of the International Theological Commission "on
human progress and Christian salvation", in *La Documentation catholique* 1726 (Sept. 4–18, 1977): 1761–68. Since these
pages were written a number of episcopal declarations from
the bishops on the same topic have been issued. One should
also refer to the discourse of John Paul II at the start of the
Puebla conference in January 1979 and also to his encyclical
Redemptor hominis, of March 4, 1979. Cf. Michel Sales,
"L'Homme à la lumière du Christ, l'anthropologie christo-
logique de *Redemptor hominis*", in *Communio* (May–June,
1979), 79–88.

III

NATURE AND GRACE

1. CONVERSION

Up to now, except for a few passing remarks, our considerations have been rather abstract, in fact doubly so, because, while seeking to define the relationship between nature and the supernatural, we followed the method used for so long in classical theology and considered this relationship in its most general terms, in its original indeterminate state. The "supernatural" we have been considering has not assumed (as we mentioned above) the specific traits of the biblical alliance or of the Christian mystery.[1] Furthermore, since we made use of what Paul Ricoeur once called "the method of innocence", we also left out the consideration of man's actual, present condition, which

---

[1] Cf. Henri Bouillard, "L'Idée de surnaturel et le mystère chrétien", in L'Homme devant Dieu (Paris: Aubier-Montaigne, 1964), vol. 3, 153–66.

is one of sinfulness. In fact, the abstract character of our discussion was not complete. It could not be complete because on the one hand it is obviously the Christian mystery, as faith has received it in its concrete reality, which set off in the Church this reflection on the supernatural end of man, and also because, on the other hand, in a presumably innocent creation not this world nor society nor the Church would be what they now are. Still, for the sake of a clearer analysis, it was a good thing to proceed step by step, and we think that abandoning all "scholastic abstractions" in theology, in order to launch into a synthetic and concrete exposition from the start, would not be without its disadvantages. Thus, we began by saying that our supernatural vocation was, on God's part, a gratuitous calling; next we sought to make clear how the supernatural had in fact affected man through the event of the Incarnation of God's Son and in consequence of his revelation; but this Incarnation could not yet be fully understood in its redemptive aspect because we had not yet considered the second meaning, often combined with the first, which the word "grace" has in Scripture.

"Grace" can also mean "forgiveness" [*faire grâce*]. Grace is also mercy and pardon.[2] The

---

[2] Cf. Jonah 4:2.

distinction between nature and grace in this instance is much more radical than in the case of the general differentiation between nature and the supernatural. It no longer suffices to say that the supernatural is something altogether different from a prolongation or a fulfillment of nature, something entirely different from the indispensable help nature needs to attain its profoundest desires. Between sinful human nature and divine grace we have not only a dissimilarity, a heterogeneity between two orders of being, an infinite distance that man alone cannot bridge. There is an antagonism, violent conflict (*"natura filii irae"* says St. Paul). Between grace and sin the struggle is irreconcilable. Consequently the call of grace is no longer an invitation to a simple "elevation", not even a "transforming" one (to use the traditional words); in a more radical fashion it is a summons to a "total upheaval", to a "conversion" (of the "heart", i.e., of all one's being). Faith, says Maurice Clavel very appropriately, restores our being "by overturning it completely".[3]

The expressions which previously designated the transition from the condition of a creature to that of a son of God—from "nature" to the "supernatural"—come back to mind here with a

---

[3] M. Clavel, *Ce que je crois* (Grasset, 1975), 290.

new and stronger meaning. We have already had to say that there is an "incommensurable" abyss between one order and the other; and passage from the first to the second can be accomplished only by the overthrow of the "old man with his old nature", so that a "new heaven" and a "new earth" can come to birth. We had already been convinced that "no one can see God without dying". But how much more should we believe this now! If everything based on man alone is fragile and impermanent, and consequently deprived of hope, given the inevitable limitations of all creatures, how much more sombre will the perspective be "if one thinks of the sin of pride, of self-sufficiency which inevitably gnaws away at all man's accomplishments".[4] Before it can be

---

[4] Jean Bastaire, "Le Socialisme à l'épreuve de la foi", *Feuillets de l'amitié Charles Péguy* 214 (Jan.–March, 1977): 13. Péguy, who as we know made much of the "mysterious connection between the temporal and the eternal", did not fail to observe also "the profound . . . differentiation between the temporal and the eternal": "Un Nouveau Théologien", in *Oeuvres en prose, 1898–1914*, ed. Marcel Péguy, Bibliothèque de la pléiade 114 and 122, 2 vols. (Paris: Gallimard, 1957), vol. 1, 1073. His thinking is not simplistic. Cf. above, 112. And quoting Pascal on the greatness and the wretchedness of man he goes even further: "Whoever forgets either the one or the other is equally mistaken, if one likes, or, if one must choose, whoever forgets the wretchedness is making an infinitely

"transfigured" our sinful nature must first be "turned inside out".[5] This is the summons which re-echoes from one end of the Scriptures to the other. We hear it at the beginning of the Gospel, and it reverberates in Peter's first missionary sermon at Jerusalem: Μετανοήσατε![6] This is much more than a simple invitation to "contrition" or to "doing penance" for particular thoughts or actions. The inner change that must accompany the hearing of the Good News "affects all the dimensions and penetrates even to the depths of one's existence".[7]

In this new vision of things, which is the only truly concrete one, we might say in summarizing that if the union of nature and the supernatural was brought about in principle by the mystery of the

---

greater mistake": "Deuxième Suite de notre patrie", in *Oeuvres en prose*, vol. 1, 189. Cf. Françoise Gerbod, in *Feuillets de l'amitié Charles Péguy* (Oct.–Dec., 1979): 244.

[5] "God will in the end be reached only in a gesture of turning": Pierre Teilhard de Chardin to J. Mortier, Feb. 15, 1940. Idem, Dec. 8, 1939: "It is mainly the notion and the gesture of this turning which remains to be discovered, in the light of desire and of prayer." This is something doubly true when we need to break with "the powers of evil": idem, *Le Milieu divin* (Paris: Seuil, 1957), 188.

[6] Mk 1:15; Acts 2:38.

[7] Cf. Karl Lehmann, "Sommes-nous encore capables de nous convertir?" in *Communio* (Sept.–Oct., 1978), 2–7.

Incarnation, the union of nature and grace can be fully accomplished only through the mystery of the redemption.

Still, according to Catholic teaching, which on this point differs from that of Luther and Calvin, our sinful nature is not completely corrupted by sin. Freedom, that prerogative of man created in God's image, was wounded, but not destroyed, so that grace in its triumph will not reign over a helpless enemy; it will not have to displace man, but free him from his slavery. Thus, in a second stage, and by God's initiative, a new relationship will be established between nature and grace, no longer one of antagonism but of union (synergy— συνεργία, as the Greeks say). This is not the place to go into the lengthy debates on the history of the differing positions adopted by the two great Latin Doctors of grace, St. Augustine and St. Thomas Aquinas. We might merely observe that the most usual difference between them, an essential difference but not a contradiction, arises because St. Thomas frequently begins by considering human nature as such in the abstract, independent of sin and its consequences; whereas St. Augustine takes as his starting point the experience of sinful man. While fully recognizing the transcendence of the supernatural, St. Thomas (giving perhaps a somewhat too facile interpretation of the *fecisti nos ad Te* of St. Augustine) "considers it as a completion bestowed on nature in the direction towards which its active inclinations already tended".[8] Still less do we need to venture into the thicket of subtle problems which confront whoever wishes to particularize this union, this "cooperation", or the process of the rebirth and development of human liberty under the action of grace. It is quite reasonable to assert that many of the discussions on this point—e.g., the famous debates *de auxiliis* in the seventeenth century, which the pope sought in vain to forbid, or the never-ending quarrels over Jansenism—were mostly fruitless, not only because too much party prejudice and too much that was merely "human, too human" was involved, but more basically because on both sides these discussions were inspired by an attempt to rationalize the problems, with too little respect for the mystery. We will not say that at the bottom of these quarrels certain serious spiritual trends were not involved.

[8] Guy de Broglie, S.J., "Autour de la notion thomiste de la béatitude", in *Archives de philosophie* 3 (1925): 222. See also the works of Etienne Gilson. Blondel's teaching mentioned above (43–44) seems to me to bring in at this point a desirable complement. As for St. Augustine, "that so-called pessimist", as H.-L. Marrou says, "he loves to stress the final blessing which even sin itself has not abolished": *Théologie de l'histoire* (Paris: Seuil, 1968), 33. Cf. Augustine, *De Civitate Dei*, 22, 24, 1.

However, a certain professional "curiosity", surely more naive than perverse and yet stigmatized by the great spiritual writers, is a vice to which theologians were exposed in every century and one which they did not always resist.[9] Still, the fact remains that one cannot declare the second distinction between nature and grace "out-of-date" any more than the first one, without at the same time affirming that the entire economy of Christianity has fallen into desuetude.

It is all the more surprising, then, that an author who pretends to write seriously should ingenuously ask, in his eagerness for reforming everything, for a "modification" of the "meaning of grace", a modification which would demand many others, especially the radical transformation of the entire "sacramental system", which, he says, is kept going today only thanks to a "distortion" that cannot be justified; he also wants a "revision in depth" of the entire liturgy; he calls for an entirely "new language" which would finally make it possible to "state the faith and the mystery of salvation". This "profound refashioning", he maintains, is "indispensable" if we wish to go beyond the mere "surface reforms" that have been

[9] Cf. Erasmus' satire in the *Praise of Folly* against the "theologasters" of his time: *Opera Omnia* (Leyden, 1906), vol. 4, cols. 463–65.

accomplished so far and to draw the true conclusions that flow from the "intuitions of Vatican II".
The Council would in fact oblige us (although
it says the exact opposite) "to redefine all the
realities of Christian faith". "Even the notion
of salvation itself" needs "to be reexamined";
however, this process, the author concedes, does
not mean that it will have to be "liquidated";
we hope that the same will be true of the "Our
Father", although the latter's incomprehensible
language will have to be sacrificed. This is a
sweeping program indeed, to accomplish which
we are invited to show two kinds of courage:
"courage to admit that religion has changed" and
"the courage to move ahead" (move ahead, it
seems to us, on the wide path and the easy way);
for "any halt in the movement would be a turning
back, a bogging down, a sign of death"; but
if we go ahead on this new "exodus", then, O
marvellous promise, "the Holy Spirit's role will
be renewed". [10]

[10] Henri Denis, *Des Sacrements et des hommes* (Chalet,
1975), 30–57. The author at least lets us hope (11) that the
sacraments "will never come to coincide entirely with human
ideologies". He is also willing to admit that "it would not be
fair to lay all blame for the reaction", provoked by "fear",
"on the shoulders of a pope or an ecclesiastical group": idem,
Les Chemins de la théologie dans le monde de ce temps (Centurion,

After that we shall be less surprised at the even more radical offensive launched by men like Ernst Bloch, whose atheism, while decked out coquettishly in biblical and Christian allusions, always remains militant. One notes, however, that this offensive is based on a scientific and sociopolitical analysis which remains very superficial, or, to tell the truth, entirely arbitrary. "Out of what soil", asks Bloch, "did the notion of grace grow?" And he replies:

> On one side there is a Lord; on the other, his humble servants. The Master shows them favor; they accept this grace with gratitude and lick his boots. . . . Certain religious categories like that of grace were formed in camps where there reigned this dehumanization, this degradation of men, this insult to their dignity. We have come a long way since then. . . . Is there any place for grace anymore? Do we not need a new category to express whatever it was that grace was supposed to mean?[11]

Now that slavery and superstition have been vanquished, now that the universe, finally recog-

---

1977), 78. We are mentioning these books only as instances of a whole literature of propaganda, well-meaning no doubt, but properly speaking, nonsense.

[11] Ernst Bloch, "Dialogue avec Gabriel Marcel", in *Présence de Gabriel Marcel* (Paris: Aubier-Montaigne, 1979), sec. 1: "Gabriel Marcel et la pensée allemande", 62.

nized for what it is thanks to the "cosmological revolution", has become "a republic", and we ourselves have been liberated from the Caesars, the doctrine of grace no longer has any meaning for us, and it is our duty to reject it as something degrading for us. . . .[12]

Are such words worthy of a philosopher? One might be pardoned for supposing that they were uttered by some benighted scientist trying to speak like a politician. They are certainly not the words of a historian, of any man at all aware of the specificity of spiritual realities. Here, all the orders are jumbled up. And if Bloch does happen to possess some light on man's present condition, in which grace might offer him some help, he resists the temptation of admitting it by telling himself that in our present wretched state "we still do not know what man really is". But at the same time he forbids this man whom he wishes to exalt to look for any way of reaching a superior destiny, now or later, and padlocks him into a strictly "this-worldly" sphere, as one of his interlocutors observed.[13] Still, such a prejudice in favor of total autonomy is not enough to do away once and for all with the double experience of mankind which Christian revelation brought out into the open.

[12] Ibid.
[13] Ibid.

One cannot so arbitrarily reduce the relations between man and God to those between a slave and his Caesar. One cannot so easily choke back man's double aspiration by which he seeks to respond to a transcendent call and thereby before all else to be delivered from evil. We find the perfect answer to Bloch's caricatural analysis, and to the claims he makes based on it, in these lines which Philippe Nemo had published a year earlier:

> That man has a master must be hell for him, if he has to struggle in the net of impotence before this master. But it can be blessedness, if man's acceptance of the master's benevolent purpose leads to his own deliverance from a fallacious autonomy, which only means abandoning himself to dispersion in the world; if it calls him back to the ties of sonship which teach him the dignity of being delivered from the world.[14]

2. ALLERGY TO SIN

If someone declares that he is allergic to "grace", the reason is that he is first allergic to the very idea of sin. Intimidated by the reigning ideologies, some Christians think they should banish both words from their vocabularies; but they encounter

[14] Philippe Nemo, *Job et l'excès du mal* (Grasset, 1978), 180–84.

considerable embarrassment when they try to find equivalents for them. For in fact the thing they do not want to face is the very reality conveyed by these words, even though they are only half conscious of this. Their objections to the language of the Church brings up here something more than a practical problem of "adaptation" or "acculturation". And one cannot fail to see that some of these people are so sensitive to certain claims advanced in the name of the "human sciences" or of "modernity" that they have abdicated all their critical spirit, and bury themselves in speculations which lead to a very superficial and very uninspiring concept of man himself.[15]

Such notions, which claim to be very scientific—this sort of neutral optimism—show little resemblance to the reality that strikes every observer less wrapped up in "science". They cannot bear comparison with the profound views that a centuries-old experience, still valid today, suggested to so many men of genius, even those who were ignorant of our faith or who did not share it. (But for these nihilists, does the very idea of genius or heroism or sanctity still have any meaning?)

Certainly, in the strict meaning of the word, sin

[15] On the contrary, "humble humanism admits to sin": Edward Schillebeeckx, *Approches théologiques* (Brussels and Paris: Éditions du C. E. P., 1967), vol. 3, 85–87.

is a biblical and Christian idea; it presupposes not only the authority of some transcendental law, but also a personal relationship between man and a personal God. "When a man can commit a crime without its being a sin", declared Péguy, "then he is not a Christian."[16] "Faith in Christ and in his redemptive death is what really teaches man what sin is, its grievousness and the depths to which it affects human existence. Thus it becomes abundantly clear that sin is not only a relative imperfection, but a rupture; not just a mistake, but a breaking away from God that divides man against himself."[17] Sin, we might say, is one of the elements in the Christian economy; and outside of that economy it cannot be fully understood. So let us not be surprised at seeing so many men, even some who live highly moral lives, who misunderstand sin. There was as much naiveté as good will in the question proposed not long ago by an excellent review: "How shall we present the idea of sin so that it may be credible?" Christian faith does not exist piecemeal; and any effort to "adapt" this or that element in it to nonbelieving interlocutors in order to justify it to them runs the risk not only of remaining barren, but of producing the opposite effect.

[16] Charles Péguy, "Un Nouveau Théologien", in *Oeuvres en prose*, vol. 2, 1078.

[17] Bouillard, "L'Idée de surnaturel".

The revelation of God is also the revelation of man. In the darkness of a still-unformed conscience, does not remorse for a culpable act or one considered as such re-echo like the voice of the divinity? But the full revelation of what sin is cannot be separated from the revelation of the God of Abraham, of Moses and of Jesus Christ.

> It is before God and only before him that we come to realize the darkness in which we allow our minds to pine away, our minds which really long to know nothing but him,
> And if his pure light had not rested on some of our forefathers . . . ,
> we would never have known that we needed to be saved,
> because we had betrayed ourselves into sin and cast ourselves into the night which we believed was day![18]

One might even advance the paradox that the full realization of what sin is does not exist in the sinful Christian, however lucid he may be, but only in the repentant Christian.

> It is our relationship with God which makes our fault clear, and shows it as a fault that has been left behind. There is no knowledge of sin save in the pardon we receive for it. Even when the prodigal son came back to his father's house, he could not

[18] André Frossard, *L'Art de croire* (Grasset, 1979), 84–85.

say the words, "I have sinned" until he had been reassured by his father's action. Sin is not so much something that cripples us as something from which God's love for us delivers us. He is the liberator; that is the only thing that matters. But there can be no liberation unless we are delivered from something. That "something" is sin.[19]

Pascal cries out: "I open my arms to my Liberator"; but we can hear Jesus silently answering him, "You would not invoke your Liberator unless you had already encountered him." And indeed this is what he meant and what he noted in his Memorial: "In proportion as you expiate them (your sins), you will come to know them." Is this not what enables us to glimpse another paradox, an even more amazing one, but one that we cannot call into question: namely, that the one who understands sin best is not the sinner, not even the pardoned sinner, but the saint?

However, one does not in the least need to be a Christian to understand or even simply to feel and see, despite all the efforts at camouflaging it, that evil is inherent in our human condition.[20]

[19] Alain Cugno, *Saint Jean de la Croix* (Paris: Fayard, 1979).

[20] "Each time", writes Proudhon, "that humanity attains a higher revelation of itself, it strikes horror to its heart": *Confessions d'un révolutionnaire* (Rivière, 1929), 19. One should

How vain does a certain "scientific" pretension appear compared with the notion that emerges from the Old and the New Testament! "There lay the world, corrupt in God's sight, full of oppression; and God saw the world so corrupt. . . ."[21] The Deluge did not suffice for long to purify it; the whole succession of the Scriptures testifies to this. From their Master the disciples of Jesus learned "what was in man".[22] If the Gospel is indeed the Good News, and the only good news that man needed to hear, it is precisely because in order to recover hope man needed to learn that the double obstacle confronting him, the weakness of his nature and the evil ingrained in his condition, was conquered. If it is true, absolutely true, as a sharp-tongued critic made it a point to remind us recently, that God "has given us not a spirit of fear but a spirit of love", it is no less true, and the Gospel is there to prove it, that Jesus never hid the austere side of his message; and that the refusal to recognize this or any effort to blur it can only give rise to a miserable caricature of that "spirit of love".[23]

---

make allowances for the author's tendency to use very trenchant language.

[21] Gen 6:12.

[22] Jn 2:25.

[23] On the Christian idea of sin, I refer the reader once and

However, our purpose here is not to start a scholarly discussion. Let it suffice to observe that if anyone refuses to accept these two correlative terms, sin and grace, in their simple and usual meaning, even if he claims to be and is an exponent of an "evolved" Christianity, of an "adult" Christianity more in tune with "modern thought", he would very evidently be contradicting the tradition of ancient Israel, as well as that of the Church who in her liturgy reminds us of these facts every day. Worse yet, it is this entire tradition and really all of Scripture and Christianity as a whole that would be denied if one tried to do away with the drama between sinful man and the God who offers him grace. To say this does not authorize any pessimism; it does not follow that our awareness of sin should turn into an obsession or become the ruling preoccupation of Christian existence. Quite the contrary, it is the indispensable condition for entering into joy. "All alike have sinned; all alike are unworthy of God's praise. But God proved how well he loves us in that while we were still sinners Christ died for us."[24]

---

for all to the excellent work of François Bussini, *L'Homme pécheur devant Dieu: théologie et anthropologie* (Paris: Cerf, 1978).

[24] Rom 3:23; 5:8. Cf. *Gaudium et spes*, 13. "Jesus does not come first of all to tell us what to do; he comes first of all to

A darksome drama, this, and not to be dissembled, this drama of sinful humanity. A bloody drama, the climax of which is Calvary. This climax too is bloody, for "without the shedding of blood there is no remission of sin". But in the eyes of faith there is a luminous conclusion, the joy of reconciliation, a return to life. For the sacrifice of Christ abolished definitively the powerless inventions of man who had always sought for expiation and pardon; it is capable of bringing salvation to all.[25]

This needed to be said because the ideology in whose name the very notion of sin is being rejected tends to penetrate, whether it be only as a result of calculated reiteration, into Christian consciences. Thus, a recent book, which could be considered semi-official, cited the words of the eucharistic Consecration but left out the final words, "for the forgiveness of sin".[26] Again, as Fr. Bernard Bro,

---

pardon, because man needs God's pardon. . . . The preaching of the Gospel in the Church, as far back as one can go, always based the call to conversion on the pardon of sin brought to us by the risen Lord. . . . Jesus rises again in order to pardon . . . but the experience of pardon refers us back to the days before Easter": Jacques Guillet, "Jésus avant Pâques", in *Les Quatre Fleuves*, 4:35–36. By the same author, see *Les Premiers Mots de la foi* (Centurion, 1977), 62–66.

[25] Heb 9:28

[26] Cf. Mt 26:28; Rom 4:25. The same formula has been left

O.P., observed, certain constantly repeated appeals for mercy "conceal an unadmitted petition; people would like not to need mercy anymore; it conceals a revolt against the idea that, as sinners, we really need salvation." Again, a new type of "pharisaism manages not to hear any mention of pardon and reconciliation, for instance in the sacrament of penance, because that would reveal both our sin and our wretchedness."[27] Such people like to quote Jesus' words: "Neither will I condemn thee", but they omit what follows: "Go, and henceforth sin no more."[28]

Following another avenue of escape, which seeks its justification in a grandiose theory, there are those who wish to recognize only collective sin, "objectivized" sin, "social" sin, i.e., the sin committed by others. A universe is constructed where evil is everywhere denounced, but nowhere admitted; where it is always endured, never committed.[29] By thus "transferring the evil which is in man to the evil in the structures"—called "structures of sin"—one is led, in addition, to the

---

out of many of the "creative" credos that have been imposed upon the faithful.

[27] Bernard Bro, *Le Pouvoir du mal* (Paris: Cerf, 1977), 140.

[28] Jn 8:11.

[29] Cf. Georges Chantraine, "La Vérité du sacrement de pénitence", in *Communio* (Sept.–Oct., 1978), 13.

idea that man is essentially good, and that it is only society which corrupts him, and that he has no need of conversion of heart.[30] Sometimes such people invoke to the point of foolishness the idea, certainly a Christian one, of collective salvation, of the "salvation of the world"; but they forget that "no matter how closely we are bound up with one another in our development and our consummation *in Christo Jesu*, we still remain, each of us, a natural unity, with responsibilities and incommunicable possibilities."[31] It is important, then, to remind ourselves that "sin is something eminently personal; in a way it is the most personal thing there is; hence our avowal of guilt must be personal also, and God's pardon must reach down into the depths of our heart, of our sinful conscience, to convert it."[32]

---

[30] On this point see the profound study, showing as much sympathy as critical acumen, by Karl Barth on Rousseau, *Images du XVIIIᵉ siècle*, trans. Pierre Godet (Neuchâtel and Paris, 1949), 79–155. Rousseau does not envisage a true conversion of heart, but he does "discover" that the heart exists (cf. 142–43). Still, as Barth recognizes, "if we understand what Rousseau never seems to have grasped, that nobody can live from anything but pardon", it is not possible for us to cast a stone at him (126).

[31] Teilhard, *Le Milieu divin*, 178–79.

[32] Msgr. Coffy. Cf. Mk 8:16. On the sacrament of penance, read the articles by G. Chantraine, Christophe von Schönborn

This is one of the key ideas, one of those most threatened in our times, that John Paul II considered it necessary to stress in his first encyclical:

> We cannot forget that conversion is an interior act of peculiar depth, in which the individual cannot be substituted for by anyone else; the community cannot "replace" him. . . . In the long run it is necessary that this act be a step taken by the individual himself, in the profoundest recesses of his conscience, with a complete realization of his culpability and of his trust in God, when he places himself before God like the Psalmist and confesses: "I have sinned against thee."[33]

---

and Michael Gitto in *Communio* (Sept.–Oct., 1978). Cf. Hans Urs von Balthasar, "Jugements", in *Communio* 3 (1980): 20–29.

[33] Encyclical *Redemptor hominis* (March 4, 1979), no. 20. In the final statement of the Latin American bishops approved by the Pope at Puebla, the expression "system of sin" is replaced by "system marked by sin". "This was not done by chance, and the substitution indicates something more than a shade of meaning. . . ." The former expression, in fact, had become current in Latin America to designate "institutionalized violence"; but it had "the serious drawback of stressing structures, not men . . ." (François Francou).

3. EVIL AND HISTORY

When faith in God disappears,

since one can no longer lay the blame on the God whom one denies, the responsibility for evil should fall back on man. But some eliminate that culpability by saddling all the blame either on neutral factors presented as laws of history, or on certain objective adversaries. Thus, the subject of history is really only the subject of the original impetus. But since such a hoax cannot last forever, the subject of history, man, will abolish himself when he has to admit that the guilt is his. Then they speak of the "death of man". The Gospel exorcises such sorcery. . . . Its message can be accepted only by the man who recognizes himself as a sinner. The movement (which pretends to be a liberating one) is all taken up with the future and accepts the death of innocent people as the price of the expected happiness. But in this they subject history to a sort of law of natural selection and deny it as truly human history. On the contrary, the salvation offered by Christ comes about in an act of solidarity with those who have been crushed.[34]

[34] F. Bussini, *Revue des sciences religieuses* (Strasbourg, 1976), 261. He sums up an article by J. B. Metz, "Quaestiones Disputatae", in *Erlösung und Emanzipation* 61 (1973): 120–40.

The basic sin, of which the thoughtful man seeks in this way to justify himself in atheism, is "believing himself innocent". What he proclaims is not just his individual innocence, but the innocence of man, that great being who, in his successive representatives down the ages, "creates history" and divinizes himself as he divinizes history.[35] Compared with this grandiose undertaking, who cares about the inevitable waste products? "If Alexander, Caesar and Napoleon had been ready to become tender", demanded Engels, ". . . what would have happened to history?"[36] Whoever reasons like this takes his place without any remorse of conscience, whether it be with pride or modesty, in the footsteps of the

[35] "The divinization of the future" as Nikolai Berdiaev called it in *Le Sens de l'histoire*, French trans. S. Jankélévitch (Russian ed., 1916; French ed., Paris: Aubier-Montaigne, 1948), 80. See also Maritain's expression, "*chronolâtrie*", a word which, as Etienne Gilson remarked, "deserves to become immensely popular" because "the spiritual vice that it designates is everywhere at work" in our times.

[36] Karl Marx and Friedrich Engels, *Werke*, vol. 6, 279; cited by J. D'Hondt, *De Hegel à Marx* (Paris: P. U. F., 1972), 197. While more open to humane sentiments, Michelet was not far from espousing similar ideas when he stated he was ready to "see a miserable caste of insignificant people-machines" being sacrificed to bring about the progress of all: *Le Peuple*, ed. L. Refort (Didier, 1946), 58–59.

Alexanders, the Caesars and the Napoleons. He takes his place in the army of humanity which goes marching on. . . .

Such then, beyond every shabby refusal to admit one's individual culpability, is "the great proclamation of innocence", raised to the level of a universal principle, whose poisonous fruits we are tasting already. Promising to lead us to the definitive liberty of our species by the only effective way, this proclamation "flatters us on every side". M. Philippe Secrétant who observed this does not for all that hesitate to say that it seems to him to "contain the substance of sin". For in fact,

> when the science of psychological and social alienation thinks that it has penetrated the mask of evil and presents itself as the source of salvation, it becomes, while pretending to de-mystify sin, the accomplice of the sin which it denies. Perhaps that is the collective sin in which we are invited to participate. That is the sin against the Spirit, which, it is said, is unpardonable. The power of insinuation that evil possesses is shown in our history; and the supreme ruse we must discover in this evil is that it presents itself as the power which will deliver us from the alienation of our sins.[37]

[37] Philippe Secrétant, "Connaissance empirique de la culpabilité, spéculation sur le mal, confession du péché", in *Le Supplément* (March, 1977), 73.

We have some sober warnings here. At least, let us recognize that one must treat the individual person with deep contempt if one sees in him nothing more than the raw material over which one can dispose in view of constructing the humanity of one's dreams, or if one deals with him willy nilly simply as a representative of a "race" or a "class" and loves or hates him as such. We cannot justify or excuse this latter attitude even if we declare that "the hatred of persons" is not "willed in principle";[38] that it reaches them "only in so far as they are the personifications of economic categories" and consequently of "alienating and oppressive social relationships". That would indeed be to compound the evil, for it means authorizing oneself (nay, obliging oneself) to hate for such formal reasons a much greater number of persons, while keeping a good conscience about it because in these persons one hates only the system that they represent. And so the empire of hatred spreads. Let us also try to understand, in examining ourselves, that we must be very unskilled in interior analysis if we identify the consciousness of sin with a morbid "guilt feeling" which should be combatted, or if we mis-

[38] Cf. Alfred Ancel, former Auxiliary Bishop of Lyons, *Dialogue en vérité: chrétiens et communistes dans la France d'aujourd'hui* (Editions sociales, 1979), 162, cf. 165.

take the spiritual evil within us for a psychological flaw, and thus expect to rediscover the right path not through contrition, but through therapy. At this point many learned considerations drawn abusively from psychoanalysis or sociology may try to bedazzle us. Even though they cannot always pretend to possess scientific exactness these disciplines can be a valuable help to us by making us see in greater detail some of the hidden mechanisms by which, as we already knew in general terms, our nature is conditioned; but if we imagine that by such means we shall succeed in penetrating into the depths of man's being, we shall be acting like sophists.[39]

The new scientism which flourishes in our day is picking up the torch from that of the last century, or rather it runs on a parallel course with it. Its procedure consists in drawing from the "human sciences" the same sort of unwarranted conclusions that the earlier one drew from the "natural sciences". For instance, in the past, going beyond the limits of their competence with a really inexcusable lack of circumspection, certain men convinced themselves and tried to convince their contemporaries that thought was nothing but a secretion of the brain, merely because the anatomy

[39] See below, section 4, 155.

of the brain had achieved great progress. Other learned men, amazed by the discoveries about the origin of species, too hastily concluded that there was no essential difference between humans and the other animal species; and if their reflections led them to conclude in favor of generalized evolution, they thought that by this step they had relegated belief in a creator God to the realm of myths. The theologians who today are tempted to line up behind what have been called (a bit too smugly) the conquests of human sciences would do well to meditate on these precedents. It would be wise for them to ask themselves whether it does not sometimes happen that some of the qualified representatives of these sciences, no matter how admirable their discoveries may be, venture out into territory which does not belong to them. The theologians can thus reflect on the fact that the fundamental realities, those in which or in relation to which man is involved, will always escape these positive studies, and this is true all the more as these disciplines make real progress in their "scientific" character.[40] It will be of some help for

[40] "The mind of man", said Auguste Comte, "considered in itself, cannot be a subject of observation": letter to Valat, Sept. 24, 1818, in *Correspondance générale* (Mouton, 1973), vol. 1, 58–59. Cf. my "Morale e mistica, l'antropologia tripartita nella tradizione cristiana", in *Mistica e mistero cristiano* (Milan: Jaca Book, 1979).

the theologians to observe also that if any one of these branches of learning is obviously incapable by itself of fully accounting for man, there would not be much hope of succeeding in this endeavor by appealing to all of the branches of learning put together, so long as each one of them seeks to make such totalitarian claims.

To take one example with many applications, in man there is a difference between his *psyche*, his *nous* and his *pneuma*. This last designates, in the biblical and Christian tradition, a region very different from the *psyche*; a region which cannot be explored by the investigations of positive science, but by a spiritual experience which it is arbitrary to neglect as though this were nothing but a dreamworld which disappears in the sunlight of scientific progress. It would be to oversimplify or rather to suppress an enormous problem, if one reduced to one and the same thing the unconscious of the *psyche*, probed by so-called "depth" psychology, and the profound recesses of the *pneuma*; in practical terms this would be to deny the latter while ignoring it, and to end up (as one writer has) by assimilating the spiritual joy of a St. Francis of Assisi to the (consciously or unconsciously) calculated pleasure on which Bentham has constructed his theories. It is not psychoanalysis or any other type of "psychology" which we should accuse of narrowness or blindness; but only the kind of "positivism" which barricades the universe of man within what pertains to these disciplines.[41]

We are not, therefore, underestimating any of the conquests of experimental science, or despising the research which we owe to them—either in the human domain or in that of nature—when we remind ourselves of the necessity of considering

[41] One should keep in mind that the positivistic attitude as regards science which Freud always maintained owed nothing to his discoveries. See for instance his *Correspondance avec le pasteur Pfister, 1909–1939*, eds. Ernst L. Freud and Heinrich Meng, trans. L. Jumel (Paris: Gallimard, 1966), 172. The question becomes more involved here because, as a result of one of those peculiar games of musical chairs of which the history of word use offers us many examples (in theological language, consider the complete change in the meaning of the expression *corpus mysticum*), here "soul" [*l'âme*] and "mind" [*l'esprit*] have changed places. When Paul Claudel wrote his famous parable of *animus* and *anima*, he would have had to reverse the meaning he gave to each of these two words if he had wished to speak like St. Paul, distinguishing *psyche* and *pneuma*. It is true that if he had done so he could have only presented us with a rather different parable, since while exchanging meanings the two words would have also taken on new shades of meaning. One might also mention, regarding the *psyche*, the fine book by M. André Forest on *L'Avènement de l'âme* (Paris: Aubier-Montaigne, 1977). (In a previous book, Forest described *La Vocation de l'esprit* [Paris: Aubier-Montaigne, 1953]; on 181 he used a traditional term, reemployed by Maurice de Guérin: "the divine mirror of the soul".)

all things *in their own order*. Scientific research has opened up before us immense new horizons, and will do so again—but in its own order, which is not the only one that exists. It operates successfully only in consequence of a twofold abstraction of principle: abstraction from all value judgments and from the question of being itself. From the merely practical point of view, it would be well for us to reflect on the ideas suggested by the author of a *Théologie de l'avenir*. Alluding to a famous case which long antedated those we have been mentioning, Dr. E. L. Mascall remarks: "There remains much work for theologians to do, but they will face a very difficult situation if we leave them as their heritage a theological system as deeply conditioned by twentieth century perspectives as the theological systems we inherited were conditioned by the persuasions of the period before Copernicus."[42]

In short, the *De Profundis* and the *Miserere* remain invulnerable to the best verified results of science; they spring from an experience which science can neither provide nor undermine; they are no less real today than they were in the past, and they will not be less so in the future.

[42] E. L. Mascall, *Théologie de l'avenir*, French trans. Delteil (Desclée, 1970), 163.

Will they finally become irrelevant, obsolete for all and for all time—as they may already now be for some choice spirits—when that radical "mutation" of man has been brought about, an event which many prophesy with a tone of anticipated triumph, while on the contrary others make us fear it as the worst threat to our species? This, as in the question of the "supernatural", was the conviction of Ernest Renan in his youth. One can hardly read without embarrassment what he wrote in 1848, in *L'Avenir de la science*:

> Moral evil characterizes only one phase of humanity. . . . I am a man of culture; I find no evil in myself, and spontaneously I pursue in all things what seems most beautiful to me. If all men were as cultured as I am, all of them would be like me, fortunately incapable of doing wrong. . . . The *educated* man needs only to follow the delightful bent of his inner impulses; he might adopt the slogan of St. Augustine and of Thélème: "Do whatever you *like*", for he could only want beautiful things.[43]

Should one merely smile at this adolescent pipe dream, the product of a fevered brain? Or was it really nothing but an adolescent dream? Under an apparently less "elitist" form, does the same de-

[43] Renan, *L'Avenir de la science*, 2nd ed. (1890), 354–55.

lusion not still haunt the minds of a certain number of our contemporaries? When people abandon the absolute norm of the good, along with belief in God, are they not near to condoning, closing their eyes if they must because they are too delicate, the outrages committed against the human herd today in the name of an elitism of the future?

4. REALISM

"What I find very strange in the attitude of many Christians today", wrote Henri Gouhier a few years ago with his habitual restraint of expression, "is that they seem to have lost sight of a fundamental notion, that of sin." And yet, as Jean de Fabrègues remarked after him, "this notion, which has grown so vague in the minds of Catholics, is so essential to the universe that in the last half century it has been reappearing everywhere, in all current literature, from Kierkegaard to Georges Bataille." (Académie des sciences morales, 1973, 2, 62–66.) "*Miserere mei, Deus, secundum magnam misericordiam tuam. . . . Amplius lava me ab iniquitate mea. . . . Tibi, tibi soli peccavi. . . . Averte faciem tuam a peccatis meis. . . . Cor mundum crea in me, Deus!*" This plea from the depths of man's conscience, this fundamental sentiment, this *realism* is certainly not proper to a sophisticated intellectual;

nor to someone who "has stayed put". It underlies the welcome offered to the divine revelation of pardon, by which natural revelation is deepened and by which man finally succeeds in understanding himself. Everywhere, Newman observed,

> [religion] is based in one way or another on the sense of sin. . . . All its multiple varieties proclaim or imply that man is in a degraded, servile condition; that he needs expiation and reconciliation and a profound change in his nature. . . . How shall we explain the mystery of evil save by saying that there is an irremediable rift, a chronic state of alienation between God and man? . . . Without the sense of sin, for man as he is, there is no genuine religion. Moreover it would only be a masquerade, and this is why the so-called religion of civilization and of philosophy is such a great fraud.[44]

The Freudian religious novel owes nothing to Freud's clinical analyses, but derives, in its depths, from the old spirit of positivism which reigned

[44] John Henry Cardinal Newman, *Grammaire de l'assentiment*, French trans. M. M. Olive (Brussels and Paris: DDB, 1975), 475 and 481–83. This religion "which is so curiously called natural", as Pierre Burgelin also remarks, whereas "it is proposed as something resulting from culture": "Réflexions sur la religion naturelle", in *L'Homme devant Dieu* (Paris: Aubier-Montaigne, 1963), vol. 2, 321.

at the end of the last century; it has not taken anything away from the truth of these profound remarks of Newman.

This obscure recognition of the state of sin—however crude and unsophisticated may be the forms it adopts in what we call primitive religions, however aberrant the practices invented to deliver men from it by appeasing the divinity for them—will always be one of the indispensable conditions for recognizing man in his concrete situation, i.e., in his true greatness as well as in his wretched state. Why is it that today some churchmen take such pains to avoid reminding man of it? Are they afraid that it might shock "the modern conscience"? Do they fear to be pitied or made fun of? Why do they no longer dare, ever, to say that there is *also* a "world" which is accursed? Why is sin never anything more than an "error" or a "failure" on their lips? They are shabby imitators of Tolstoi, who, in the *Réunion des quatre évangiles*, translated the expression "forgiveness of sins" as "deliverance from errors". Pointing out that little detail, Pierre Emmanuel concluded very rightly that this "sufficed to show how far Tolstoi was from the Christian religion", even though he maintained some of its moral precepts. In the same way, he continues, "Tolstoi was, in the strict sense, a usurper of the messianic morality in the name of the instinct for self-deification that exists in every man and that was so powerful in himself, driving him, in 'saving' himself, to 'save' others from their 'errors' ".[45] The clerics whose timidity we deplore are certainly not guilty of the sacrilegious audacity which Pierre Emmanuel discerns in the unconscious of the great novelist who changes into an evangelist. But do they not understand that by their soothing words they run the risk, contrary to their intentions, of engendering in souls which are not frivolous a deeper pessimism than that which they are afraid of—deeper because it is without hope? One day, chatting with his friend Janouch, Kafka said: "What, then, is sin? We know the word, but we have lost the feeling for it and the real understanding of it. And that, perhaps, is damnation, dereliction, the absurd."[46]

---

[45] Pierre Emmanuel, *La Vie terrestre* (Paris: Seuil, 1976), 138. Cf. 205: "Sin—this word indicates an absolute experience that a being has of himself with reference to absolute reality. It implies an experience of a totally different kind than psychological guilt; it designates the dimension proper to spirituality. It is not psychic unbalance that causes the greatest saints to declare themselves the worst of sinners. It is instead spiritual realism. Their intuition, their wisdom, their longing for fullness reach out at the same time towards the depths of human wretchedness and towards the summit of enlightenment."

[46] Gustave Janouch, *Conversations avec Kafka, les lettres*

If sin is not sin, then who will set us free from it? And what meaning can be given to the revelation of Mercy?[47]

Certainly, this same realism has another side to it. It invites us to recognize that we are frail creatures, that we do not know what we do, and that the sinner is first of all a wretched being. It reminds us that the Creator knows full well the sort of clay he has fashioned us from and that the Redeemer has come to heal the sick, open the eyes of the blind and deliver the captives. If we timidly dare to think this applies to ourselves, then, in imitation of the One who willed to be the Good Shepherd, must we whom he has sent out to others not always bear this in mind even more? God forbid that we should ever forget it! But God forbid, also, that we should ever forget the other side of that same truth!

In his brief spiritual testament, read at his funeral (April 24, 1970) from the pulpit in the temple of the Oratory in Paris, Pastor Marc Boegner had

---

nouvelles (Paris: M. Nadeau, 1978), 168. One should also read what follows, which is more humane in tone and in its manner of being applied.

[47] It is surprising that in the translation of the new Mass, in the second Canon, we find *omniumque in tua miseratione defunctorum* rendered as "and all the departed".

dictated these words: "There exist two fundamental verities, sin and grace. . . . My sin, yes, my sin; but also grace: that is the essential truth which never abandoned me throughout my long life." And a few days before this, with his fading strength, he had written in his own hand: "The word grace is certainly the one which sums up all the marvels which, during the last seventy years, I discovered little by little in Jesus Christ." Such a brief summary can obviously not suffice to give an adequate view of the Christian mystery; and this testament did not propose to do so. One can also judge that the Calvinist tradition was reflected in the statement; but it would be a mistake to see in it a sign of that hypertrophy of the sense of evil which has often (not always wrongly) been reproached in certain expositions of Christian doctrine. Nothing would subsist anymore of the Scriptures which the Church transmits to us in their integrity— nothing of any ecumenical hope for reunion among Christians for whom this treasure is a common good—if these words "human nature", "sin", "liberty" and "grace" were rejected or simply overlooked; if the realities which they designate were flatly opposed or insidiously watered down. One could scarcely speak, then, even of a "castrated Christianity": incapable of resisting the assaults of every adverse power, as Alexander Solzhenitsyn expressed it recently after some months spent in gloomy contemplation of our "Christian" West.

The realism we need does not consist, evidently, in seeing in the evil that men do an example of pure sin, for none of our liberties is pure liberty. Each of us can feel within himself many natural impulses, "whose morbidity is in part curable by biological or psychological therapy"; but the illusion consists in carrying things to the extreme. This gives one a vision of the world that fails to recognize "the original and specifically spiritual character of man's moral makeup". It fails to recognize this when it sees in him nothing but "a natural being" whose "interior mechanism" could be repaired by some technique just as easily as a "badly functioning machine". Whether we consider man as a social being or as an individual, objective science would suffice to discover the laws governing him; and the application of those laws through appropriate techniques would be able to create perfect individuals organized in perfect societies. Such a delusion, which would radically destroy every notion of sin or liberty, destroys man's dignity at the same time. And since it conflicts with reality,[48] the monstrous

---

[48] All the plans that aim at "the total abolition of evil", as Etienne Borne remarks in *Le Problème du mal* (Paris: P. U. F.,

effects it produces, moreover, are in proportion to
the progress made:

> The power that technology confers on man, over
> himself and over nature, being of itself ambiguous,
> its growth during the twentieth century has pro-
> duced results diametrically opposite to those which
> had been expected. Instead of safeguarding the
> primary human values and insuring their attain-
> ment, it handed them over to an ever greater
> threat. Psychological, sociological and political
> technologies make it possible to crush persons, to
> invade their privacy, to fragment our cities and
> subjugate peoples. Our biological, chemical and
> physical technologies threaten the health of indi-
> viduals and even the existence of the human
> race. . . .[49]

The tongue is the best thing in the world, or the
worst. The technologies derived from modern
science are neither the one nor the other. But they
are an instrument that can produce the best or the
worst results. In the hands of a sinful man, who
renounces his liberty when he denies his sin,
they become effective instruments for his self-

1958), 115, "go bankrupt" one after the other, and their
"liquidation" provokes "crises of nihilism".

[49] Gaston Fessard, *Libre Méditation sur un message de Pie XII*
(Plon, 1951), 28–33.

destruction; not merely of external enslavement
which can be accompanied by the cruellest ill-
treatment, but of inner degradation which does
not always spare the executioners any more than
their victims. But still this poor humanity, weak
and sinful, will always win out over technology,
we have the certainty of this in Christ; and even
now, day after day, humanity triumphs over
technology secretly (we have proofs of this in
the miracle of certain spiritual resurrections).
Humanity is a marvel, wounded yet indestructible, which finds the meaning of its liberty in the
confession of its guilt.

5. LIBERATION AND SALVATION

The distinction which we outlined first of all
between nature (created) and the supernatural has
been paralleled by a second distinction which
completes and specifies it concretely: the division
between nature (sinful nature) and grace. This
latter distinction, reinforcing as it does the former
one, enables us to understand better how diverse
are the two realities whose juxtaposition or opposition, confusion or separation have led to so
many arguments during these last few years.
Whatever may be the nature of the links estab-

lished between them, it has become customary to designate these two realities by the expressions: "man's liberation", and "salvation in Jesus Christ".[50] The latter is clear because it refers directly to the Christian faith; the former, on the contrary, is full of ambiguities because it can be understood in different ways depending on how one conceives of man. In this single word "liberation" one can, for instance, include "social liberation" and also a total "liberation" in the metaphysical order. This latter would mean the breaking of all ties between man and God, considered as an oppressive force; and the former kind of liberation might be looked upon as the condition for the second. Even if we understand the word in the former sense exclusively, *"the* liberation" can also, in its abstract and general sense, designate some sort of undetermined ideal which does not take into consideration the limitations of all sorts without which no viable society can exist and which must be respected if true liberty is to be guaranteed. So, it is always important to ask: liberation from what?[51] However, without ex-

---

[50] In liturgical language, where ambiguity is not a problem, the two words are used interchangeably. Thus, in the great antiphons during the days preceding Christmas we find: *Veni ad liberandum nos, veni ad salvandum nos*, etc.

[51] That is why, without proscribing the word "liberation",

amining diverse and ever-changing situations, or the many problems of social philosophy which might be raised at this point, we shall take the word "liberation" in its most legitimate, most incontestable meaning, as it is quite commonly found today in the official language of the Church, where it is distinguished from "salvation". We must say, then, that this "liberation of man", understood as a social emancipation, is a human undertaking which, even when inspired by views of faith, brings about (or seeks to bring about) by human means certain changes in the organization of temporal society, and which becomes part of human history, with all the hazards, the uncertainties, all the threats too (and perhaps the reality) of a regression, of going from bad to worse, which will always remain possible in this groping and sinful world.[52] "Salvation in Jesus Christ", on the contrary, is essentially a divine undertaking which comes about in the depths of hearts and is inscribed in eternity; it is "the bringing about of

---

it might be good to replace it in certain cases with a more positive term, e.g., "human advancement".

[52] "One never knows how things will turn out", as Etienne Gilson wisely observed in *Les Tribulations de Sophie* (Vrin, 1967), 154. Examples of such unexpected happenings, little and great, are all around us.

God's Kingdom in a free being".[53] We saw this earlier, in the second chapter, while speaking of the transcendence of (supernatural) salvation over all the purposes at which man has a right to aim in order to organize the earthly city as best he can. This makes clear the proper role of the Church; she is the messenger and bearer of this salvation and hence she cannot be assimilated, either in her structure or in her aims, to any of our human societies. But now we must say more.

To be saved, man must first be freed from his own sins, *liberated from himself*, for "whoever commits sin is the slave of sin".[54] This law applies to the entire human race as well as to each one of its members; and this liberation is, in Christ our Redeemer, the work of God's grace.[55] This is what St. Paul, embracing an even wider per-

[53] Such is the definition given by Edmond Barbotin at the conclusion of a close study of vocabulary in *Foi et langage* (1979), 34. See also Gérard Soulages, *Epreuves chrétiennes et espérance* (Paris: Téqui, 1979), 151–86: "Libération de l'homme et salut en Jésus-Christ".

[54] Jn 8:34: πᾶς ὁ ποιῶν τὴν ἁμαρτίαν δοῦλός ἐστιν.

[55] See W. Kasper, *Jésus-Christ*, trans. J. Désignaux and A. Liefooghe (Paris: Cerf, 1976), 99 and 140, and on 123: "Salvation in the Kingdom of God consists essentially in the pardon of sins and in the joy of encountering God's immeasurable and undeserved mercy."

spective, teaches in the Epistle to the Romans where he shows all of creation yearning to be "delivered from the slavery of corruption in order to enter into the liberty of the glory of the children of God." This liberation, to which all aspire who have already received the "first fruits of the Spirit", is also called salvation.[56] Thus the same word, liberation, can in the long run be taken in an integral meaning, very different from but not less extensive than the meaning which it assumes in the systems founded on atheism.

Few sophisms are more insidious, more apt to perpetuate or even to reinforce the bonds which impede all liberation, even the merely social variety, than the identification of conversion of heart with religious individualism—as if one had to renounce the call of the absolute which re-echoes in the depths of one's personal conscience in order to escape the illusions and sterility "of a religion where individualism is king"! This is another instance of those false dilemmas in which a coercive system of thought pretends to imprison us, a system of thought which appears to have given up all efforts towards rationality. One may well be frightened at seeing such an aberration spreading

[56] Rom 8:18–24.

among certain groups within the Church itself. Is this not the parallel, or rather a copy (thank God still a somewhat pale one), of what the communist leader Piatakov taught: "A true Bolshevik must submerge his personality in the collectivity"? Is not the value of the "new man" gauged, among people like him, by "obedience to the Party line, which has become an absolute norm"? And should we not on the contrary admire those who under the most difficult circumstances have succeeded in preserving or in recovering their interior conscience?[57] A society for which and within which one could no longer conduct oneself personally according to justice and truth, but where, under a false pretext of efficiency, one would have to let oneself be dragged along blindly by a collective current would never be a society of free men. For that very reason there exists a first link, a very close one, between the two orders of liberation referred to above: social liberation itself can only succeed if the "hearts" of those who seek it are freed by an inner "conversion" from the massive pressures and the pure criteria of efficacy.[58] On

[57] Cf. Hélène Zamoyska, "Réflexions sur les problèmes de l'intériorité en U.R.S.S.", in *Axes* (Feb.–March, 1973), 55–56. See also *Gaudium et spes*, nos. 16 and 17.

[58] It is tempting to give way before superior numbers, or

the other hand, this social liberation, even supposing that it has been brought about as perfectly
as possible, would still be far from constituting a
satisfactory solution for man if he had to remain
imprisoned in the narrow confines of his earthly
horizon. Even that is saying too little. Without the
perspective that Christian faith opens of a "way
out", leading to divine transcendence and a per-
sonalizing union with God in Christ, humanity
will not only always remain far from the goal it
seeks; it will condemn itself to despair.[59]

It is not, then, in order to avoid one or the other
of the two tasks which demand our efforts that we
have to distinguish carefully between the two
realities signified by the one word "liberation".
On the contrary it is in order to harmonize them
better, to show more clearly their necessary con-

---

before the strength of an opinion that seems to possess the
guarantee of success. But whoever yields to such a temptation
against the dictates of his conscience introduces a germ of
death into the work with which he is associating himself.

[59] This is what Fr. Teilhard de Chardin often repeated,
although he has been so lightly described as an unguarded
optimist. Cf. my *Teilhard posthume* (Paris: Fayard, 1977),
especially chaps. 4 and 5. See the symbolic story of the "Great
Monad" in his *Ecrits du temps de la guerre*, 2nd ed. (Paris: Seuil,
1976), 261–78; also G. Cottier, *La Mort des idéologies et
l'espérance* (Paris: Cerf, 1970), 11–12.

vergence and to avoid entering upon unilateral paths which would only lead us down blind alleys. In conclusion, let us recall the teaching of the Gospel; its supernatural light will not dictate to us the details of our acts, but it must guide us in all things.

> Jesus does not speak of the evils in the social order as springing from a social disorder which could be overcome by means proper to that social order. He refers them to the idea of sin, that is to an interior evil, an offense against God. The prophet Amos, when he "roared out" against the abuses of his time, was not protesting in the name of human dignity which was being violated, but in the name of the sanctity of God which sin outraged. Human dignity and human justice, separated from God, end by becoming corrupt. They deteriorate very quickly, even when the abstract notion of them persists. The entire Gospel is filled with this idea of the presence of sin in the world. . . . Christian optimism springs, not from the belief that the man who is good can be shielded against the external circumstances which might make him become wicked, but from the conviction that God can bring about a transformation in him, in the depths of his being. He can be "converted"; his heart can be changed.[60]

[60] Yves de Montcheuil, *Le Royaume et ses exigences* (Editions de l'Epi, 1957), 47–49.

Basing itself on this Gospel teaching which it is bound to safeguard, the magisterium of the Church reminds us of the pressing duty which the word liberation points out to all of us in our varying situations.

The Church has a duty to proclaim liberation to millions of human beings, the duty of helping to consolidate this liberation; but she also has the corresponding duty of proclaiming this liberation in its full and deep meaning, as Jesus announced it and brought it about.[61] Freedom from everything that oppresses man, but especially freedom from sin and from the Evil One, in the joy of knowing God and being known by him. Liberation made up of reconciliation and pardon; liberation derived from the fact that we are God's children, that we can call him "Abba", Father, in virtue of which we recognize in every man a brother whose heart can be transformed by God's mercy. Liberation which urges us by the power of charity to communion in which we find the summit and fullness of that communion in the Lord. Liberation which must overcome the various slaveries and idols that man forges for himself and makes the new man grow to his full stature.[62]

[61] Thus we must neither dissociate nor confuse the proclamation of the Gospel and the task of human development. Cf. John Paul II, allocution to the bishops of Santo Domingo.

[62] John Paul II, *Discours de Puebla* (1979), chap. 3, no. 6. Cf.

The Gospel does not tell us that the world is evil—the Creator's handiwork is good—but it does say that "the world lies in the power of the Evil One" (1 Jn 5:19).[63] Jesus did not come to establish a social program that would result in "a better world"; not that he condemns the search for such a program, but his mission belongs to a different order, and whoever rejects that mission will in the end make the former search vain. He has come in person to found "the new world".

"And thou, child", prophesied old Zechariah, the father of John the Baptist, "shalt go before the Lord . . . to give his people knowledge of salvation (γνῶσιν σωτηρίας), through the forgiveness of their sins (ἐν ἀφέσι ἁμαρτιῶν αὐτῶν) by the merciful kindness of our God. . . ."[64]

Le Thème de la libération, texts by John Paul II, ed. Fr. Roger Heckel (Vatican City, 1980).

[63] 1 Jn 5:10. Cf. 12:31: "Now the prince of this world will be cast out." See also 14:30; 16:11; Mt 6:13, etc.

[64] Lk 1:76–78.

CONCLUSION

In summary fashion and without appealing (at least intentionally) to theories of particular schools or to theological discussions more or less out–of–date, this simple catechesis has sought to sketch the meaning and to show the scope of this double distinction which, all mere semantics aside, must absolutely be maintained, and maintained to the full. In the most explicit and complete fashion it finds its expression everywhere in the liturgy. It is pointless to list a series of examples for either of these two notions; there are so many of them. Let us be content, then, with just one very clear example that includes both. It is found in the *Ordo Missae* as revised according to the instructions of Vatican II, i.e., what is commonly called the "Mass of Paul VI". It follows, at the same moment of the Mass, the order which we have adopted here. "*Per hujus aquae et vini mysterium,*[1] *ejus*

---

[1] We give the passage in Latin not only because of the

divinitatis (esse) consortes, qui humanitatis nostrae fieri dignatus est particeps" (nature–supernatural, in their concrete realization). *"Lava me, Domine, ab iniquitate mea, et a peccato meo munda me"* (sin–grace).

While we have considered them in succession for the sake of a clearer analysis, these two distinctions obviously must not be separated from each other. As the notion of the supernatural would remain an abstraction unless it were made concrete in the reality of the Covenant consummated in the God-man, the idea of salvation would likewise remain an abstraction without the reality of the new Sacrifice: Incarnation and redemption are inseparable for us. Human nature, in each of us, is always both created and sinful; it is always in fact the sinful man who is gratuitously called to conversion, to divine life; and it is always in fact this divine life which is gratuitously given him along with the pardon for his sins. The idea of sin is no more a simple social category than it is a simple moral category, such as a simple humanism,

---

beauty of the words but also because the translator (in French), apparently not understanding the meaning of the word *mysterium*, made the phrase banal. One can better understand "this sublime prayer", as Etienne Gilson called it (*Les Tribulations de Sophie* [Vrin, 1967], 163), if one recalls how it originally began: *"Deus, qui humanae substantiae dignitatem mirabiliter condidisti, et mirabilius reformasti. . . ."*

even theistic humanism, might accept. It is an essentially religious idea. At bottom (and this evidently does not always rise to the surface of the consciousness, which is why the malice of sin is not always grave), sin is not the simple refusal to abide by a law, even a divine law, but a refusal of God's invitation to share his life. "Natural religion", in its true, historic meaning, and not in the unreal and artificial sense given it by the philosophy of the eighteenth century,[2] is based on the sense of sin; in the obscurity of its myths it recognizes the disease, and by its rites it seeks but does not find a remedy. This remedy is given to us by the central doctrine of Christ the Redeemer. Thus, "revelation begins at the point where natural religion falters."[3] And it is in unveiling all the

[2] Most of the time this "natural religion" was "artificial and literary" (Lachelier), but sometimes it tried to be really religious, as in the case, "perhaps an exceptional one in France", of Rousseau: Henri Gouhier, in *Les Méditations métaphysiques de Jean-Jacques Rousseau* (Vrin, 1970), 47. In any event, it is only a late development.

[3] John Henry Cardinal Newman, *Grammaire de l'assentiment*, French trans. M. M. Olive (Brussels and Paris: DDB, 1975); see the end of the passage cited above, 150. His second University Sermon "examines natural religion, not as it has sometimes been considered in the abstract, but such as the history of positive religion shows it to have been. He brings out how natural religion offers corroboration of the

positive strength of that remedy (the healing of the illness being at the same time the recovery of access to divine life) that revelation also unveils how serious the evil is. This points to the added responsibility incumbent on whoever has received the revelation of redemption in the blood of Christ—the duty of fulfilling this role which has fallen to him, to share by grace in the salvation of the world.[4]

This salvation, this sharing in the divine life, was offered to man in Christ; and the Church of Christ has received the commission to transmit it to all generations. True, this offer no longer seems to arouse much interest in a certain number of people, adepts of a Christianity which claims to want to be not "moderately" but fully "modern",

---

mysterious truths concerning the fall and the corruption of mankind that revealed religion teaches": Louis Bouyer, *Newman* (Paris: Cerf, 1953), 238. Cf. the ninth University Sermon, no. 21: "Revealed religion, as such, has the nature of a positive rule which adds more or less to natural religion and which implies the revelation of facts which, without it, we would not have been able to discover" (French trans. A. Renaudin [Brussels and Paris: DDB, 1955], 205–6). See also H. Fries, "Newmans Bedeutung für die Theologie", in *Newman Studien*, eds. von H. Fries and W. Becker (Nürnberg: Glock und Lutz, 1948), vol. 1 (cf. RSPT [1951], 366).

[4] Cf. Henri de Lubac, *Catholicisme*, 5th ed., Unam Sanctam 3 (Paris: Cerf, 1952), 192–96.

perfectly adapted to a world hostile to all mystical excesses, whether moral or metaphysical. This appears in "glaring light" in the disdainful question which a theologian quotes while appearing to adopt it as his own: "Would a man with good sense today still want to become God?" What a surprising lack of ambition in this "modern" Christianity! "The question here is not at all one of refusing to identify God and man—the Fathers of the Church, and any true Christian at any time, would never think of such a thing. It is a question of indifference to the central message of the New Testament."[5] We might add that it is a question of blindness as regards man's deepest longing, a longing which is no less vehement today than it was in other times, even though it is often muted (as it was in all other times) by the immediate concerns of existence. Even in its massive apostasy, contemporary atheism is far from having renounced this longing entirely. In its most lucid represen-

---

[5] Karl Rahner, "Etre chrétien dans quelle église?" French trans. in *Jean-Robert Armogathe présente "Etre chrétien?": la réponse de Hans Küng* (Brussels and Paris: DDB, 1979), 93–94. Cf. 95: Rahner asks "whether the author still possesses an authentic and integral doctrine of grace, like that of Paul or of Jesus and like that of the entire Christian tradition", or whether all that is not "mangled" and reduced to some sort of "liberating humanism".

tatives it merely seeks, through an idolatrous inversion of roles, to become God without God. To the question posed by Hans Küng as though to challenge a doctrinal tradition which he considers out-of-date, Joseph Ratzinger, who is no fool, replies: "Yes!" He even goes on to observe that "rarely has an epoch been so determined" to become God, and he takes as an example both of this desire and of its failure the case of Ernst Bloch. The latter has

> made of the *Eritis sicut Deus* the guiding idea in his interpretation of biblical heritage turned to the future, in which the revolutionary ferment is stirring. . . . He merely formulated the deepest urge hidden behind the passion for emancipation which characterizes our century. The liberty which is desired here, a liberty which consists in getting rid of the limitations of the human condition, cannot be satisfied outside of achieving the status of the divinity, and that is precisely why its criticism is radical to the point of nihilism.

Let us conclude that "a Christianity which offers man something less than making him God is too modest. . . . In the struggle for man in which we are engaged, such an answer is insufficient."[6] All

[6] Joseph Cardinal Ratzinger, "Le Christianisme sans peine", in *Communio* (Sept.–Oct., 1978), 84–95.

along, Christianity has shown perhaps a somewhat less cheerful face; it reminds us with more
realism of our condition as sinners, and it does not
allow us to forget the prayer given to us by our
Lord: "Forgive us our trespasses . . . deliver us
from evil"; but at the same time it opens before us
the gates of life in the bosom of the Blessed Trinity.

APPENDICES

APPENDIX A

THE "SUPERNATURAL"
AT VATICAN II

Occasionally one hears that while the Second Vatican Council had of course spoken of grace, it never made use of the word "supernatural", so widely used for so long in Scholastic treatises and even in works addressed to wider audiences.

The assertion is not quite correct. As a matter of fact the word is found fourteen times in the Acts of the Council, even though an index as laboriously compiled as the one by Monsignor Simon Delacroix does not mention it at all.[1] It is found twice in *Lumen Gentium* (nos. 12 and 61); four times in

[1] Editions du Vitrail et du Centurion, 1967. "It even happens that in the French text they have substituted 'spiritual' for the original *supernaturalis* in the Latin": Msgr. Philippe Delhaye, *Note conjointe sur la nature et la grâce*, Esprit et vie (Chambray-Tours, France: C. I. D., 1978), 414, note 12. On the contrary, in the translation of *Gravissimum educationis*, the word *caelestis* was translated by the word "supernatural".

Christus Dominus (nos. 17, 20, 27 and 35); twice in *Optatam totius* (nos. 11 and 21); five times in *Apostolicam actuositatem* (nos. 6, 7, 8, 24 and 30); once in *Presbyterorum ordinis* (no. 16).[2] True, in most of these passages the word is used incidentally. The Council's language is generally concrete; it speaks more commonly of nature and grace than of nature and the supernatural, and nowhere does it take up *ex professo* the classical problem which these two words sum up and which is discussed in many theological treatises. But to the question which has been raised here it is possible to bring more pertinent answers.

First of all, it is a fact that Vatican II, in spite of the large amount of material it issued, did not, any more than any previous Council, undertake to give us a complete exposition of Catholic doctrine. Furthermore, like Trent and Vatican I, even in the passages filled with doctrine, it sought to avoid the technical language of speculative theology—without in the least suggesting any discredit of such theology. This had always been the practice of Councils; the rare exceptions consisted in a few words in specific circumstances, calculated to bar

[2] Philippe Delhaye et al., *Concilium Vaticanum II*, Concordance, index, lists of frequencies, comparative tables (Louvain-la-Neuve: Publications de CETEDOC, 1974).

the way to some incipient error.[3] Even when the
Fathers of Trent sought to define the Catholic
doctrine on the Eucharist, challenged by the new
theories of the Reformers, they showed themselves extremely prudent. Carefully avoiding the
use of the word "transubstantiation" in the definition itself of the changing (*conversio*) brought about
through the Consecration of the bread and wine,
they had simply added: "*quam quidem conversionem
catholica Ecclesia aptissime transsubstantiationem ap-
pellat*".[4] The statements made on several occasions
in the conciliar assembly leave no doubt on this

[3] One should further remark that, by the fact that it was
used in an official text, the technical term was thereby removed
from the systematic context from which it had perhaps been
taken. Cf. Jules Lebreton, "Catholicisme" and "Dogme et
critique", in *Revue pratique d'apologétique* 4 (1907); Léonce de
Grandmaison, "Qu'est-ce qu'un dogme?" in *Bulletin de littérature ecclésiastique* (Toulouse, 1905), 181–92, especially the
first part on "dogma and history".

[4] *De Eucharistiae Sacramento*, can. 2, *Denzinger-Schönmetzer*,
1652. Cf. no. 1642: *convenienter et proprie*. There is a good
historical outline in Edward Schillebeeckx, *La Présence du
Christ dans l'Eucharistie*, trans. M. Benzerath (Paris: Cerf,
1970), 23–47. The author also observes (63–64) that in the
word "we find an obvious reminiscence of the Bible's words,
of the *panis supersubstantialis* of Matthew 6:11, in certain
manuscripts", as had been remarked at Trent itself by Bishop
Jean Fonseca as well as other bishops and theologians.

score.[5] Furthermore, in spite of an opinion rather widespread today, the word transubstantiation itself, by which as early as the twelfth century authors sought to express the idea of a "substantial conversion", owed nothing at all to Aristotle.[6] In his *Declaratio Fidei Orthodoxae*, Bossuet commented on the Decree of the Council of Trent, and yet one cannot find in his text the slightest vestige of the theory of substance and accidents. Still, no Catholic author has ever been able to claim "that for the sake of peace he emasculated the strictness of the conciliar definitions".[7]

We also know that the Fathers of Vatican I turned down an entire dogmatic schema prepared by Franzelin—the first draft of what later became the Constitution *Dei Filius*—not because of the doctrine it embodied (although some questions were raised over certain points), but because they found it couched in language that was too Scholastic in tone. Moved above all by pastoral con-

[5] Cf. Augustin Theiner, *Acta Genuina . . . Concilii Tridentini* (Zagreb, 1874), vol. 1, 502, 504, 526.

[6] Cf. P. M. Gy, O.P., "L'Eucharistie dans la tradition de la prière et de la doctrine", in *La Maison-Dieu* 137 (1979): 94–97.

[7] Lebreton, *Revue pratique d'apologétique*, 194–95 and 533–34. On the nature and the authority of Council formulations, see also John Paul II, allocution to the members of the International Theological Commission, October 1979.

siderations and by a realization of what a Council should be, a number of bishops from the first asked for a complete revision of the schema. What they said came to this: it is the production of an excellent theologian working in his special branch of science, but it is too far removed from the form which a conciliar decree should assume; it sounds more like a didactic treatise; it has the tone of the classroom and one can almost hear a professor lecturing at his podium; it does not sufficiently respect the just liberty of theological opinions. So the schema was sent back to the "Deputation on Faith". There Franzelin defended his work during two sessions; but even so it was decided to establish a commission of six members, not including Franzelin himself, to recast it.[8] The new document, whose main author was Kleutgen, differed from the former one, not only in style, but in its general makeup and even in the structure of each paragraph. After one meeting of the commission, Canon Gay wrote: "The first draft has been completely rewritten and, in my opinion, much improved." Granderath, the historian of the Council, dwells at length on this episode, citing or sum-

[8] The Commission was made up of three bishops and three experts: Kleutgen was flanked by an "anonymous priest from Savoy" and Canon Gay, the theologian of Msgr. Pie (and future Auxiliary Bishop of Cardinal Pie).

marizing a number of episcopal interventions; he tends, however, to minimize the difference between Kleutgen's work and Franzelin's.[9] Fr. Henri Rondet, who reexamined the whole dossier, has presented the facts in a more balanced light, both by making use of contemporary testimony and by comparing the texts.[10]

Something similar happened during the period of preparation for Vatican II. At the opening session of the Theological Preparatory Commission in the fall of 1960, its secretary, Fr. Sébastien Tromp, S.J., clearly gave notice to all the members and experts: *"Non agitur de faciendis tractatibus theologicis, sed de constitutionibus dogmaticis."*[11] That this rule was not always happily applied by all is something we all know. Its author himself was no doubt too much influenced by his long career as a professor to keep his own rule in mind all the

[9] Th. Granderath, S.J., *Histoire du Concile du Vatican . . . jusqu'à sa prorogation d'après les documents authentiques*, ed. Fr. Conrad Kirch, S.J., French trans. (Brussels, 1908), vol. 2, chap. 7, 109–37.

[10] Henri Rondet, S.J., *Vatican I* (Namur and Paris: Lethielleux, 1962), chap. 6: "Les Travaux du concile"; the Constitution *Dei Filius*, 95–115 and Appendix B, 181–83.

[11] One bishop said the same in a session of the General Congregation (referring to a text under discussion): *"Plus habet indolis (sit venia verbo) exercitationis scholasticae quam documenti conciliari."*

time. One must also admit that the Fathers of Vatican II, for generally objective reasons, showed themselves less inclined to praise the theology of the Preparatory Commission than their predecessors had been to praise that of Franzelin; they demanded much more than changes in form or structure—but that is another story.[12]

To the two motives of a more general nature that we have just indicated[13] we think we should add another which the circumstances seemed to suggest, if not absolutely impose. It was a consideration present in the minds of a number of people, bishops and experts, who during the Council were entrusted with the task of preparing the texts or of revising them.

By its very inflation the word "supernatural" had taken on more and more extensions of meaning, which had led to abuses and misunderstandings

[12] In fact, these schemas drawn up by the Preparatory Commission were not too traditional, as has so often been said, but not traditional enough. See the intervention of Cardinal Frings on November 14, 1962, regarding the schema *De fontibus*.

[13] One may observe that the *Roman Catechism*, which was drawn up in accordance with the instructions of the Council of Trent and which contains a great deal of theology, rarely uses the word *supernaturalis*; it does not employ this word in many cases when, following the custom of the theology of the time, one would expect to find it.

like those we pointed out above.[14] In addition, for at least two centuries, it had become, in the hands of a number of unbelieving writers, a sort of label pasted onto details of the Catholic faith in a false and caricatural sense—and this regardless of whether the intention of these authors was ill-disposed or not. This had led to a whole series of new ambiguities.[15] Worse yet, perhaps, was the fact that since the sixteenth century the word had frequently been involved with a particular theory which had given rise to many controversies. One of these was quite recent; it had caused a good deal of strife, and many of the Council Fathers and theologians had it fresh in their memories. The Council therefore judged it more equitable and wiser not to use such a word in certain contexts, so as not to perpetuate certain ambiguities or stir up

[14] Jean Guitton relates, in his *Paul VI secret* (Brussels and Paris: DDB, 1979), 69–70, that one day the Pope said: "An elderly priest published a book against *tedious theology*; it had no literary value, but in it I recall that he criticized the too frequent use of the word 'supernatural'."

[15] Cf. Henri de Lubac, *Surnaturel: études historiques*, Théologie 8 (Paris: Aubier-Montaigne, 1946), pt. 3: "Histoire du mot surnaturel", especially the last section. Many other examples might be mentioned. "Current English usage usually associates 'supernatural' with 'ghost stories' ": Bernard Lonergan, "La Mission et l'Esprit", in *Experience et Esprit: Mélanges Schillebeeckx*, eds. Paul Brand et al. (Paris: Beauchesne, 1976), 156.

old quarrels again by seeming to canonize or at least to favor one school's theories (called the theory of "pure nature", which presupposed two final ends for man).[16] By doing so it gave proof of a sense of tradition, so sadly disregarded today. More precisely, Vatican II showed a reflex similar to that of Vatican I, where the Fathers, without excluding the word *supernaturalis*, had expressly refused all allusion to that hypothesis of "pure nature".[17]

By acting thus Vatican II avoided a possible

[16] I discussed this distinction in various passages of my book *Surnaturel*, and also in *Augustinianisme et théologie moderne* and *Le Mystère du surnaturel*, Théologie 63 and 64 (Paris: Aubier-Montaigne, 1965). See in particular, for the current situation, the preface to the latter volume. I restudied the question in line with the teaching of the Constitution *Gaudium et spes*, and taking into consideration some modifications of the question, in *Athéisme et sens de l'homme*, Foi vivante 67 (Paris: Cerf, 1968), especially chap. 2: "Sens total de l'homme et du monde", 91–150.

[17] Granderath, *Histoire du concile du Vatican*, 115, 135, 143–44, and the final texts themselves. Cf. Msgr. Philippe Delhaye, "Histoire des textes de la constitution pastorale", in *Vatican II, l'Eglise dans le monde de ce temps*, Unam Sanctam 65 (Paris: Cerf, 1967), 269. "In an interview published by *La Croix* on September 30, 1965, a member of the Central Committee said very plainly, 'We need to oppose the idea of two human vocations, one supernatural and the other natural, more or less juxtaposed to each other. What matters is the integral human vocation.' "

obstacle to ecumenical dialogue; as we know, semantics have not always been a negligible quantity in religious controversies. The word supernatural itself sometimes arouses antagonism among the followers of the Reformers; and on the other hand it ran the risk of awakening all kinds of echoes from a certain Lutheran orthodoxy which is still known as "supra-naturalism", a trend common especially in Germany in the eighteenth century,[18] and with which nobody wishes to be associated today. In the Eastern churches the word was never in common usage and the theory to which we have been alluding was even less so.

Be this as it may, the fundamental distinction between "human nature" and the "supernatural", a distinction which underlies their union brought about by grace as we have tried to explain it here, remains a fundamental element in Catholic doctrine. So it is not surprising that, just as in the liturgy,[19] it is to be found everywhere in the Council texts themselves in other terms and under many aspects and in many places very explicitly and concretely. We shall quote some examples here:

[18] Cf. Frédéric A. Lichtenberger, ed., *L'Encyclopédie des sciences religieuses* (Paris: Sandoz et Fischbacher, 1877–82), vol. 11, 754–55.
[19] See Conclusion, above.

Constitution *Lumen Gentium*, no. 2: "*Aeternus Pater, liberrimo . . . consilio . . . homines ad participandam vitam divinam elevare decrevit.*"[20]

Idem, no. 3: "*Venit igitur Filius, missus a Patre, qui nos in Eo . . . elegit ac in adoptionem filiorum praedestinavit.*"[21]

Idem, no. 7: "*Dei Filius, in natura humana Sibi unita . . . hominem redemit et in novam creaturam transformavit.*"[22]

Idem, no. 48: "*Ecclesia, ad quam in Christo Jesu vocamur omnes et in qua per gratiam Dei sanctitatem acquirimus, etc.*"[23]

Constitution *Dei Verbum*, no. 2: "*Placuit Deo, in sua bonitate . . . notum facere sacramentum voluntatis suae, quo homines per Christum . . . in Spiritu sancto accessum habent ad Patrem et divinae naturae consortes efficiuntur.*"[24]

[20] "The eternal Father, by an absolutely free determination . . . decided to raise man to communion in his divine life."

[21] "The Son came, therefore, sent by the Father who had chosen us in him . . . and predestined us to an adoption as sons." Cf. no. 9.

[22] "The Son of God in the nature which he had united to himself . . . redeemed man and transformed him into a new creature."

[23] "The Church, to which we are all called in Christ Jesus and in which we acquire holiness by God's grace. . . ."

[24] "It pleased God in his goodness . . . to make known the mystery of his will, thanks to which men, by Christ . . . have

Idem, no. 6: "*Divina revelatione Deus Seipsum atque aeterna voluntatis suae decreta circa hominum salutem manifestare ac communicare voluit, ad participanda scilicet bona divina, quae humanae mentis intelligentiam omnino superant.*"[25]

Pastoral Constitution *Gaudium et spes*, no. 22.2: "*Cum in Eo (Christo) natura humana assumpta, non perempta sit, eo ipso etiam in nobis ad sublimen dignitatem evecta est.*"[26]
Idem, no. 22.4: "*Christianus autem homo . . . primitias Spiritus accipit, quibus capax fit, etc. . . . Per hunc Spiritum . . . totus homo interius restauratur. . . .*"[27]

Decree *Ad gentes*, no. 2: ". . . *Libere creans et insuper gratiose vocans nos ad Secum communicandum in vita et gloria, etc.*"[28]

---

access in the Spirit to the Father and become sharers in the divine nature."

[25] "By divine revelation God has willed to manifest himself and communicate himself, as well as the eternal decrees of his will concerning the salvation of mankind, and to give man a share in the divine blessings which surpass all that the human mind can conceive."

[26] "Because in him human nature was assumed, not absorbed, by that very fact nature was raised in us also to a sublime dignity."

[27] "The Christian . . . receives the first fruits of the Spirit, by which he becomes capable. . . . By this Spirit the whole man is interiorly renewed. . . ."

[28] "[God] created us freely in his immense goodness

Idem, no. 10: "*Mysterium salutis vitamque a Deo allatam. . . .*"[29]

Idem, no. 12: "*Ita . . . elucere incipit mysterium Christi, in quo novus homo apparuit. . . .*"[30] Cf. no. 21.

Decree *Gravissimum educationis*, *Proaemium*: "*Cum . . . Ecclesia . . . integram hominis etiam terrenam cum vocatione caelesti connexam curare debeat. . . .*"[31]

In short, the Council, which in many ways affirms the divine vocation of mankind and the gratuitousness of this call, does not seem to feel the need, in order to maintain this gratuity, of calling upon the hypothesis of "a purely natural order", complete in itself. It never "speaks of man as God's creature without reminding us that his Creator" destines him "to be united with himself in Christ"; "the two notions of creation and of vocation to divine communion are always associated."[32] By thus avoiding (it was certainly

---

and mercy and in addition called us graciously to share with him his life and his glory . . ."

[29] ". . . The mystery of the salvation and the life brought to us by God. . . ."

[30] "Thus begins to shine forth the mystery of Christ, in whom the new man appeared. . . ."

[31] "The Church . . . must take an interest in the totality of man's life, including his earthly concerns, in the measure in which they are bound to his heavenly vocation."

[32] Jean Mouroux, "Le Concile et le sens de l'homme", in

done on purpose) the language of the "two different orders", as it was used in one whole
theological school (and without pretending to
exclude it either), the Council "assumed a very
important position". Indeed, as Jean Mouroux
wrote, "if there are in the universe varying levels
of analysis (creation, sin, redemption), there are
not two different orders of reality, but only one,
that of the Covenant which had creation for its
first act; and Christ is its Alpha and Omega, its
beginning and end; and this order is supernatural."[33]
That is why "when man is left without divine
assistance and the hope of eternal life, his dignity
undergoes a serious assault." But "the Church
knows very well that her message is attuned to the
secret depths of the human heart when she defends
the dignity of man's vocation and restores hope
to those who no longer dared to believe in the
grandeur of their destiny. . . . The mystery of
man is not truly illuminated save in the mystery of
the incarnate Word."[34]

L'Ere des ordinateurs: le dialogue de l'homme et de la machine,
Centre catholique des intellectuels français, Recherches et
debats 57 (Paris: Fayard, 1966), 144 and 149.

[33] Jean Mouroux, "Sur la dignité de la personne humaine",
in *L'Eglise dans le monde de ce temps* (Paris: Cerf, 1967), 232.
This in no way contradicts what Pascal said of the "three
orders", since the word "order" is not used in the same sense.

[34] *Gaudium et spes*, nos. 21 and 22.

APPENDIX B

THE "SACRAMENT OF THE WORLD"?

I

In one of his books, modestly entitled *Approches théologiques*, published in French by Editions du C. E. P. (Brussels and Paris) in 1967,[1] Father Edward Henri Schillebeeckx, O.P., wrote:

The Church manifests, as in a sacrament, what grace, the *eheyeh asher eheyeh*, is already accomplishing everywhere in human-existence-in-the-world.

In this context it is fitting to quote one of the most felicitous passages in the Constitution *Lumen Gentium*: "In Christ, the Church is as it were the sacrament, i.e., the sign and instrument, of intimate union and of the unity of the entire human race" (Introduction, no. 1). The Church is the "sacrament of the world". Personally, I consider this declaration as one of the most charismatic that have come from Vatican II. It stands

[1] Edward Schillebeeckx, *Approches théologiques* (Brussels and Paris. Editions du C. E. P., 1967), vol. 3, chap. 2, sec. 1, pt. 3: "L'Eglise sacrement du monde".

out all the more since it is found again—as though all its consequences had been felt spontaneously in advance—in the Pastoral Constitution on the Church and the world (pt. 1, chap. 4, no. 42). . . .[2]

The Church, the form in which the progressive sanctification of the world shows itself explicitly (as a profane reality) by the law of the living God, is at the same time an intrinsic aspect of the history of this world sanctified by God's unconditional "Yes". . . .

. . . . The deepest secret of what grace is accomplishing in the profane world, in virtue of the unknown and hence unexpressed name of God, is *named* and proclaimed by the "Church of Christ" and practically heralded in the witness afforded by her works. This is why belonging to the Church should be accompanied by an active will, full of hope, to change the face of the world through love for men. . . .[3]

At first this passage is difficult to understand. The quotation from *Lumen Gentium* with which

[2] The Church, says the author, "is the effective sign—the sacrament—of the union or the 'community' of all humanity in and by its union with the living God; she is the community of men living in communion with God who is life, the living one. In this universal communion the Church plays a sacramental role, i.e., she is the sign that brings this about. . . ." As Paul VI said at Hong Kong on December 3, 1970, "The Church is a sacrament of unity and of love."

[3] Schillebeeckx, *Approches théologiques*, vol. 3, 145–47.

it opens is correctly translated, except that two words, not unimportant ones, have been left out: "*cum Deo*".[4] But we must suppose that this is only an oversight of no great weight. The quotation is also carefully commented on. But is it indeed this conciliar statement that the author considers as "one of the most charismatic that have come from Vatican II"? At first he was satisfied to point out in it "one of the most felicitous passages" in *Lumen Gentium*. Is he not rather talking about that other affirmation which in the meantime managed to slip in and which he also (rather strangely) puts between quotation marks, i.e., that "the Church is the 'sacrament of the world' "? The reference that follows to the Constitution *Gaudium et spes* (which repeats the text from *Lumen Gentium*) would tend to resolve our doubt in favor of the first hypothesis, for it is accompanied by an explanation, a very accurate one, of the "efficacious sign", the "sign that brings about what it signifies", which is the Church. But to tell the truth, one does not see too clearly what is so very "charismatic" about this wise and traditional reminder of what the Church

---

[4] *Lumen Gentium*, chap. 1, no. 1: "*Cum autem Ecclesia sit in Christo veluti sacramentum seu signum et instrumentum intimae* CUM DEO UNIONIS, *totiusque generis humani unitatis. . . .*" See the very beautiful explanation of this passage by Michel Sales, "Pourquoi l'Eglise du Christ est une et comment elle le demeure", in *Axes* (June–July, 1979), 3–17.

of Christ is, and of her universal mission. But then, almost right away, we are told insistently—by an unexpected reduction of the ordinary meaning of "sacrament"—that the role of this Church of Christ is only to "manifest" a "progressive sanctification of the world (as a profane reality)", a sanctification which seems to take place without her. She only needs to "name" and "herald" what grace "is accomplishing in the profane world". This second explanation, moreover, seems more in keeping with what had been said previously, and frequently repeated, about the "desacralization" necessary for the benefit of the "original profaneness of the world"; and this second explanation corresponds better than the first to the formula about "the Church, the sacrament of the world".[5]

How these two explanations, given to us in the same context, can be harmonized, we find it difficult to perceive. The developments which follow, like those which precede, seem to invite the reader to choose the second. For it is certainly the second explanation that justifies the epithet "charismatic", bestowed on a conciliar text; it is also the explanation that allows one to sketch out, on the basis of the authority of the Council, a process of "secularization", the new "stage in the

[5] Schillebeeckx, *Approches théologiques*, vol. 3, 138 and 147.

historical evolution of Christianity"[6] (what will the next "stage" be?), from which "there will arise a new type of Christian" (what type?); this is, finally, what will make it possible to understand the Church as the "sacrament of the world", namely, as the author specifies, "as the pregnant visibility, the manifest presence of a communion *already* brought about among men".[7]

Still, a problem remains; or rather, our perplexity has grown deeper. For nowhere in the documents of the Council, either in *Lumen Gentium* or in *Gaudium et spes* or elsewhere, have we been able to

[6] Cf. ibid., 142, where the author discusses the "movement of desacralization" which "accompanies the entire history of Christianity" and "forms an intrinsic part of Christian being".

[7] Ibid., 146 (italics added). It seems to me that one ought to say as much about Jesus, not in his eternal being, but in so far as he has entered into history; he does not seem to have brought anything new with him save that he shed light on the "progressive sanctification" that had started at the beginning of the world. On 145 we find a more moderate formula (the first sentence of the text cited above). However, an even clearer explanation is given in 1967 (*Approches théologiques*, vol. 4, 284): "The acknowledgment by Christians of the world's autonomy and of its non-Christian emancipation are inextricably linked in the entire phenomenon which we call contemporary secularity. . . . Some consider secularity, not as a transformation of our relations with the world, but wrongly—as a secularization of religion itself."

discover this "charismatic formula" adopted as a title in the pages which we have been analyzing: "The Church, the sacrament of the world".

One reason for the ambiguity of this text seems to us to be a certain confusion (not always easy to avoid) in the use of the word "world". Despite some interesting efforts to restrict its meaning, the word here designates sometimes nature outside of man, sometimes the whole of human relationships, etc. Is it not just a bit exaggerated to say, for instance, that "nature, which was formerly divinized, is today the work of man"? If we define secularization as "the passage from divinized nature to humanized nature", are we not setting up a false dilemma? In paganism, nature was divinized unduly; does this mean that in reality it will ever be totally humanized through human progress? Must we believe, in line with Promethean atheism, that man is the absolute master of nature and of history? Would even that be enough to allow us, when speaking of "constructing the world", to assimilate the building of "dams" or "lightning rods" and the establishment of a society in which there would always be "more justice, more peace, more unconditional love"?[8]

[8] Schillebeeckx, *Approches théologiques*, vol. 3, 133–48.

II

Be that as it may, the key to the enigma confronting us may be provided by the consideration of the different dates at which the various essays were written that are gathered together in the 1967 anthology.

The text we have been quoting is from 1966; it is therefore postconciliar, and refers us back to the Council as we have seen. But in the same volume it is followed by other, older documents. For the moment we shall examine only one of these, which follows immediately in the book. Entitled "The Church and the World", it is a talk given at Rome on September 16, 1964, for the inauguration of the Dutch Information Center at the Council, and which was published almost immediately thereafter.[9] The author lays down the program of what, according to him, should be the doctrinal message of the project still called, at this time, "Schema 13", the framework and definitive form of which was still being discussed. "For the world", the author states, the significance of the Council "depends entirely on what will happen to it" (i.e., to Schema 13). Now, the Church "would misjudge

[9] Ibid., 149–67.

the real scope of Schema 13 and would disappoint the world if she addressed herself to the world while considering it only as a sinful reality, entirely given over to the power of the Evil One and wholly identified with 'the world which must perish'."[10] Who could fail to agree with such a statement and with others made during this talk—even though one too often senses the emergence of a certain form of argumentation by antithesis, which easily turns into Manicheanism, a form much cultivated today even though it is "one of the most fallacious figures of logic", as André Manaranche says.[11] Again, when we were told (this was in 1966) that to "take an unconditional interest in one's neighbor", i.e., to make an act of perfect charity, is "to accept Jesus in an implicit and salutary manner",[12] it seems to us that on this score every Christian can and should agree. We also willingly recognize that "profane activities in the midst of the world are neither foreign nor indifferent to Christian life";[13] but we fail to see

[10] Ibid., 150.

[11] Cf. ibid., 151: "Formerly . . . interest in the problems of earthly existence seemed to be reserved exclusively for those who called themselves unbelievers." This is misrepresenting history too carelessly.

[12] Cf. ibid., 145, 147, 148. The author cites von Balthasar on this point and refers to the parable of the Good Samaritan.

[13] Ibid., 159.

how reminding us of these truths must lead us to recognize that the "world" is "an objective expression of the life of grace", or, in other words, that "in the present economy of salvation . . . the 'world' is an implicit Christianity".[14] We have to admit that we cannot find any very clear meaning in formulas such as these.

Yet is was on such premises that the speaker in 1964 dictated to the Council the task it had to accomplish. "Implicit Christianity" will be "the domain of Schema 13", or, in other words, "the domain into which Schema 13 introduces us is *holy ground*". "In Schema 13 one of the first tasks of the Church will then be to recognize officially the holiness of the ground on which she treads at the moment when she approaches the 'world' " of which she is the "sacrament". Hence the series of imperatives handed down from the hall of the Dutch Information Center to the Council Fathers: "The link between the vast hopes of humanity and the coming of the Kingdom *must* be the dynamic element that subtends and enlivens the entire Schema." "The great problem which *must* be placed at the very center of the Schema. . . ." "This Schema *cannot be* dominated, even unconsciously, by certain aspects of Augustinianism. . . ."[15] "The

14 Ibid., 152 and 155.
15 Whereas St. Thomas recognized the "deep causes". But

contemporary meaning of 'apostolic secularity' *must* be strongly affirmed. . . ." "It will also be *necessary* to. . . ." "Schema 13 *must* show. . . ." "In the elaboration of Schema 13 the Church *must* pursue the path she very clearly laid down in the Dogmatic Constitution on Revelation. . . ."[16] "The Church *must* humbly recognize. . . ." "Thus, Schema 13 *must*. . . ." "Schema 13 *must* acknowledge and proclaim. . . ."[17]

One cannot fail to notice in this part of the talk the solemn tone of the beginning, the bold deductions, the inclusive formulas which one might take, against their author's wishes, either for simple clichés or for a program of secularistic ideology, the imperialism of an orator who hopes to impose his ideas on the Council by arousing

---

soon St. Augustine again becomes the patron of secularization, thanks to his doctrine of creation in Christ.

[16] The process of secularization would be a consequence of the chapter on tradition.

[17] Schillebeeckx, *Approches théologiques*, vol. 3, 157 and 162–66 (emphasis added). Cf. what can already be found in "Coup d'oeil en arrière sur la deuxième session", Dec. 10, 1963, in Schillebeeckx, *L'Eglise du Christ et l'homme d'aujourd'hui selon Vatican II* (Mappus, 1965), 95: "The Theological Commission must take into consideration . . ."; and 153–55, "La Troisième Session": "Schema 13 must give solemn witness to . . .", "Schema 13 must profess all this and proclaim it joyously. . . ."

public opinion. (This should probably be ascribed to the effervescence which at this time reigned in certain circles, and from which the theologians were not always exempt.) The closing invitation "to structure the world in such a way that men may be able to live in it in *a Christian manner, in a manner worthy of men*", can only provoke agreement as broad as its formulation; and as though to put a seal on the ambiguities which characterize this talk, it ended on the false note of an incomplete quotation: "The glory of God is man who lives!"[18]

III

However, the teachings of the Council the following year turned out to be quite different. Nobody could help realizing this, and our author wished to

---

[18] The passage is taken from St. Irenaeus, *Adversus Haereses*, bk. 4, chap. 20, 7. But the quotation is incomplete and misleading. Irenaeus wrote, "For the glory of God is man who lives; and the life of man is the vision of God": *Sources chrétiennes* (Paris: Cerf, 1965), vol. 100, 2, 648–49. This passage sums up a number of others like it in books 4 and 5. In recent times the quotation has frequently been given incompletely. Thus in Charles Wackenheim, *La Théologie catholique* (Paris: P. U. F., 1977), 37–38: "It is to him [Irenaeus] that we owe the beautiful formula, 'The glory of God is man who lives.' This is, as we read again recently, an age-old adage of Christians."

take note of it. From this, one may suppose, there arose the discordancies to which we called attention in the 1966 article. We find them again, at the same date, in the communication addressed to the International Theological Congress held in Rome in September; this was published in 1967 in the *Acts* of that Congress and was reproduced in a French translation in volume four of *Approches théologiques* (1969)[19]. The title remained unchanged; it was still "The Church, the sacrament of the world". But the conciliar texts, faithfully reproduced at the beginning, all speak differently. This led the author to new formulations, more or less in agreement with one another, such as: "The Church is the sacrament of salvation for the entire world, *sacramentum mundi*"; or: "As the sacrament of salvation offered to all, the Church is the 'sacrament of the world'. . . . We can say that the Church is the active revelation of the world's existential salvation; she reveals the world to itself; she makes the world see what it is and what it can become through the divine gift of grace." After this follow a few considerations which seek to show the fundamental agreement of the two formulas, linked together in their "dialectic tension

[19] Schillebeeckx, *Approches théologiques*, vol. 4, chap. 1, sec. 3, 42–48.

which has not yet reached its solution"; then a reminder (more convincing) of the necessity for the Church to seek constantly to purify herself, in humble confidence in the redeeming grace of Christ.[20]

Along with the author we think that these Council texts, as is normal, call for "theological clarifications";[21] and we can well understand that these may be somewhat tentative. Another study,[22] drawn up no doubt shortly before the promulgation of *Gaudium et spes* but after *Lumen Gentium*, clearly reminds us "that the Church is not only a κοινωνία, a community of grace with Christ and as such the fruit of his redemption; she is also an institution of salvation, to whom have been entrusted the keys which open the gates of the Kingdom."[23] A little further on there follows an attempted explanation that displays a certain psychological insight but that might be considered somewhat inadequate because it constantly seeks to adhere to the formula "sacrament of the world":

[20] Ibid., esp. 46–47.

[21] Ibid., 145.

[22] Schillebeeckx, "L'Eglise et l'humanité", in *Dogmatique*, Concilium 1 (Paris and Tours: Mame, 1965), 57–58. This text was repeated in a new translation in *Approches théologiques*, vol. 3, 167–89.

[23] Schillebeeckx, *Approches théologiques*, vol. 3, 173–74.

. . . Without the ecclesial form given by God, in Christ, to the deep rootedness of every life in Jesus Christ, this rootedness remains "a light hidden under a bushel basket", a vacillating flame which can be blown out by the lightest breath. The ecclesial environment, strictly speaking . . . is a vital condition for perseverance which grace brings about anonymously in the lives of men.[24]

Shortly afterwards an article originally written in Dutch in 1967, whose French title is "Foi chrétienne et attentes terrestres", analyzes the first part of *Gaudium et spes*.[25] The "ecclesial community" is once more defined as the "sacrament of the world" or as the "sign of salvation for the world". No doubt, "the notion of the Church as the people of God", stressed in *Lumen Gentium*, is important; but even more important is "the theme, not yet fully developed, but really present in the Pastoral Constitution: the theme of the Church as the 'sacrament of the world' ". Still, a certain

[24] Ibid., 178. This psychological view occasions a reflection similar to the one given in the 1966 text, to which we called attention above (note 20). In the same place, on the contrary, we find this judicious remark: ". . . Abandoning religious 'practice' drags Christian life down into anonymity and in the long run provokes the ruin of Christianity." From the article "L'Ecclésialité de l'homme religieux" (1959), French text in *Approches théologiques*, vol. 3, 205–206.

[25] Given in French in *Approches théologiques*, vol. 4, 48–81.

concession to the Council's thinking is made by adding the words: "present as a sign in and for the world", an expression explained a little further on by this passage: "thus, the Church is a visible sign for the world, the sign in which the mystery of the world is revealed"; or rather, she ought to be this sign, for we must make of the ecclesial community a *sacramentum mundi*, a sign *in* and *for* the world that will reveal the world to itself.[26]

One cannot be surprised if a writer holds on to a formula into which he condensed a whole theory and which he hoped to have canonized by an Ecumenical Council. One has no right to reproach him with this, in principle, provided that he tries to explain it by referring to the texts which were in fact adopted. In this case he recalled to mind very opportunely what he had declared in 1962 on the eve of the Council's first session: "It is not one's personal views, whatever their theological worth, which need to be honored."[27] However, while recognizing that the problem was a delicate one, we may ask whether the efforts have proved entirely successful. Has the correlation of the two

[26] See ibid., 64–65 and 68–71. In these passages the preposition "for", given the explanations which follow, does not seem to be capable of meaning "in favor of the world" or "for the world's salvation" but "in the eyes of the world".

[27] Schillebeeckx, *L'Eglise du Christ*, 34.

ways of speaking been harmonized? One may, at least, opine that in itself the formula which has been maintained is not a very happy one. Above all, one may be allowed to regret that, after having been advanced so perseveringly,[28] it was finally adopted by people less concerned about the precautions with which the author had surrounded it at times, people less disposed to pay attention to his remark on "the partiality of his points of view" which, he added, "should be placed within a wider perspective".[29]

One might perhaps be allowed to prefer to these speculations about the Church as the "sacrament

[28] It is strange that "sacrament of the world" is always placed in quotation marks; this happens occasionally even in Latin.

[29] Schillebeeckx, "Malentendus au concile: le problème de la langue", in *L'Eglise du Christ*, 57. However, another pamphlet which appeared in a French translation in 1966 under the same general title as that of 1965, but which had as its subtitle "Quatrième Session: réflexions sur le résultat final" (Mappus), again quotes the same preliminary text of *Lumen Gentium* on three different occasions (46, 48 and 52) without adding to it the formula "sacrament of the world" which reappeared the following year. It is difficult to follow exactly the chronology of the author's publications during the years the Council was in session. This last text appeared in an "original edition" in Holland in 1964; but it starts with the words: "Since the Second Vatican Council came to a close . . ." and the last six pages look into "the difficulties after the Council".

of the world", sketched as we have just seen at various times without having found a really satisfactory form, the simpler and less ambitious considerations found in his earlier book on Christ, the sacrament of our encounter with God.[30] The original title of this book (in Dutch) was: "The encounter with Christ in the sacraments of the Church is the sacrament of our encounter with God" (1957). There we were told that the Church was "the earthly sacrament of the heavenly Christ" and "the institution of salvation"; "the apparition of the reality of salvation on the level of historical visibility"; she is "not only a means of salvation, she is the very salvation of the sacramental Christ", etc. This little work, which no doubt constituted in the eyes of its author a sort of early draft of the volumes which followed, also had the merit (as the French translator remarks) of showing that theological reflection must always remain somewhat provisional and approximative. This is a fact which authorizes a reader to offer some critical remarks, without for all that underestimating the interest of the author's reflections.

[30] French trans. A. Kerkvoorde, Lex Orandi 31 (Paris: Cerf, 1967). See also "Les Sacrements, organes de la rencontre de Dieu", in *Questions théologiques aujourd'hui*, French trans. Yves-Claude Gélébart (Einsiedeln, 1960; French ed. Brussels and Paris: DDB, 1965), vol. 2.

IV

It must be admitted that this word "sacrament", which has come into such widespread use in our times, occasions by that very fact a number of ambiguities which are not always easy to avoid. "In the primitive Church the word 'sacrament' was used to indicate historical events, the words of Scripture and those elements of religious worship which make known the saving action of Christ and which therefore allow the Eternal to manifest himself in time and even to become present in it, as constituting its true inner reality."[31] The application of this word to the Church, an ordinary practice nowadays and one which was encouraged by the use made of it by the last Council,[32] is not entirely free from difficulties, as Fr. Pierre Vallin observed. "The concept of the Church as a sacrament", he said, "is very difficult to handle" because it offers two diverse aspects.[33] For instance,

[31] Joseph Cardinal Ratzinger, quoted by Msgr. Robert Coffy and Roger Varro, in "Eglise signe de salut au milieu des hommes" (Reports presented to the plenary Assembly of the French Episcopate at Lourdes, 1971), 32. The word *sacramentum* in "the first centuries of Christianity was used with many different meanings": Christine Mohrmann, in *Vigiliae Christianae*, vols. 3 and 4 (1949 and 1950).

[32] Cf. Msgr. Philips, *L'Eglise et son mystère au 2ᵉ concile du Vatican* (Desclée, 1967), vol. 1, 72–74. Long ago Scheeben had spoken of Christ as "the primordial sacrament".

[33] Pierre Vallin, "En marge les chrétiens?" (Colloquy at

we read in Vatican II's Constitution on the Liturgy (chap. 1, no. 2): "From the side of Christ fallen asleep on the Cross the entire admirable sacrament of the Church was born."[34] Here, the meaning of "*sacramentum Ecclesiae*" is, of course, "the sacrament which the Church is". In the same way, the obvious meaning of *sacramentum mundi* would be, at first glance and literally: "the sacrament which the world is". But when we are also told that Christ in his visible humanity is the "sacrament of God", this expression evidently does not mean that he is "the sacrament which is God". It simply affirms that God is perceived, that in some way he makes himself visible, through Christ[35] and not that Christ is the sacrament, i.e., "the sign and

---

the Institut catholique de Paris, under the direction of O. de Dinechin, 1979), 39.

[34] "*De latere Christi in cruce dormientis ortum est totius Ecclesiae mirabile sacramentum*". The wording is taken from a Collect in the old Roman missal, the one which follows the second reading on Holy Saturday.

[35] As Fr. Schillebeeckx so rightly says in "Les Sacrements, organes de la rencontre de Dieu": "Man's encounter with the invisible God under the aspect of the visible face of love shown by that same God is what we call a sacramental encounter with God. . . . The man Jesus, the visible and perfectly human personification of the redeeming God is . . . the prototype of the sacramental signs. . . ."

instrument" by which God's salvation is brought about. The same remark applies to the relationship between the Church and Christ. Thus, in one of the prayers he composed, Paul VI says to Christ: "The Church, thy sacrament and thine instrument".[36] And in the report quoted by Monsignor Coffy it is not in the same sense (even though both are legitimate) that the text says, in turn, "the Church, sacrament of Christ who died and rose again", and "the Church, the sacrament of the Kingdom of God which is coming", or "the sacrament of salvation for today".[37]

In the collective work which they published in 1978, *Il est grand, le mystère de la foi: Prière et foi de l'Eglise catholique*[38], the bishops of France did not say that the Church is the sacrament of the world but that she is "the sacrament of salvation for the world". In this way, as during the Council, all ambiguity was avoided. As early as 1971 Monsignor Coffy spoke to the Assembly of the French Episcopacy of "the Church, the sign of

[36] November 25, 1971. In my *Méditation sur l'Eglise*, 2nd ed. (Paris: Aubier-Montaigne, 1953), chap. 6, "Le Sacrement de Jésus-Christ", 175–203, the reader can find a series of passages on this question.

[37] Coffy and Varro, "Eglise signe de salut", 35.

[38] (Paris: Centurion, 1978), 63.

salvation in the midst of mankind". We learned to pray "*ut (Ecclesia) fiat* MUNDO *salutis sacramentum*". "Sacrament for the world", says von Balthasar likewise in a recent article.[39] Twice Vatican II designates the Church as *universale salutis sacramentum*;[40] it also tells us that the Church "joins prayer and labor" (i.e., essentially "the eucharistic sacrifice" and "the work of evangelization") "so that the whole world in all its being may be transformed into God's people, into the body of the Lord and the temple of the Holy Spirit. . . ."[41] "*Ecclesia sacramentum futuri*", or "sacrament of God's Kingdom", are other very correct expressions from an eschatological point of view. In the double perspective which is precisely that of the Gospel, Fr. G. Martelet wrote: "The visible Church is the sacrament of the invisible Kingdom."[42]

[39] "The Church—and in her every Christian—shares in the salutary fecundity of the divine word for the world. A Church which was not a 'sacrament for the world' (but she is such only on the Cross) would cease to be the Church of Christ": von Balthasar, "Une Méditation . . . plutôt une trahison", in *Sources* (Fribourg, 1978), 197; also in *Axes* (Oct.–Nov., 1978), 8.

[40] *Lumen Gentium*, chap. 4, no. 45; chap. 7, no. 48; cf. chap. 2, no. 9.

[41] Ibid., chap. 2, no. 17.

[42] G. Martelet, *Oser croire en l'Eglise* (Paris: Cerf, 1979), 96.

The least that one can say, in our opinion, is that the formula *Ecclesia sacramentum mundi* appears not only insufficient but inadequate to express this doctrine. On the contrary, when we read that "Christian celibacy is, within the Church, a pregnant *sacramentum mundi*, an eloquent and understandable sign which invites all men to open themselves to religious values",[43] then in spite of the persistent incompleteness of the Latin formula, the meaning is clear, thanks to the explanation given immediately thereafter, and we have no trouble in agreeing with the author because we know full well that Christian celibacy, however "pregnant" it may be as a sign and however effective an example it may offer to the majority of men, is not an efficacious sign in the same way as the Church and the Eucharist are. But the attempts mentioned above to associate the notion of the Church as the "sacrament of the world" with that of the Church as a sign and instrument of the world's salvation can only be juxtapositions,

---

This of course does not negate the profound unity of the Church and the Kingdom.

[43] Edward Schillebeeckx, "La Vie religieuse dans un monde sécularisé" (1957); French trans. in *Approches théologiques*, vol. 4, 96.

which risk being quickly forgotten, for the sole benefit of the first formula and of the ideology which it is calculated to promote.

Sacramentum mundi: the sacrament which the world is. In this sense there is nothing more profoundly traditional. The idea can be traced to the teaching of St. Paul in the Epistle to the Romans; the invisible God "allows himself to be discovered through his works" (Rom 1:20), that is, through the *cosmos*. The whole of creation is one grand book which would suffice to reveal to man the divine wisdom, if sin had not darkened his vision. This theme was dear to St. Bonaventure, among others.[44] When one's vision is purified, the divine significance of creation reappears. For the spiritual man, as Fr. Teilhard de Chardin said, the world becomes "a divine milieu". It reveals in its depths "the divine Presence"; whence the prayer: "*Domine, fac ut videam.* . . . Make your universal presence shine forth everywhere: *Illumina vultum tuum super nos.* . . ."[45] This is surely the same

[44] Cf. my *Exégèse médiévale* (Paris: Aubier-Montaigne, 1961), vol. 4, 264–70.

[45] Pierre Teilhard de Chardin, *Le Milieu divin* (Paris: Seuil, 1957), 133–64. A reviewer of Jean Bastaire's *Court Traité d'innocence* (Namur and Paris: Lethielleux, 1977) said that it was "an introduction to the sacramentality of the world".

thing that Fr. Pierre Charles, S.J., wrote, following
St. Paul: "The divine meaning of things, the value
of all things, is what theology should show."[46]
Again he wrote:

> The Church is . . . the sacrament of the world, the
> form of the entire world's adoration, the rendezvous
> of creation restored to the Word whose work it is,
> the divine meaning of this earth, and, to sum it all
> up in the words of the Gospel, the Kingdom of
> God. . . . Her mission is to invade the entire earth
> visibly, by a pacific invasion, in order to sanctify it
> and give it once again its place in the eternal
> liturgy of offering.[47]

If the first expression might cause some surprise,
those which follow it and comment on it suffice
to give proper direction to the reader's thoughts.
Let us recall, finally, the celebrated passage in
Newman's *Apologia* where he speaks of the Chris-

---

[46] In the posthumous collection which appeared under
the title *L'Eglise, sacrement du monde*, Museum Lessianum
(Brussels and Paris: DDB, 1960), 57; cf. 58–73. The title,
selected by the editor, is not found either in the texts gathered
here or in the editor's foreword where he says, "The Church,
which is Christ, [is] the sacrament of his love for all
creation."

[47] Pierre Charles, S.J., "La Vraie Nature du devoir mis-
sionnaire" (1935), in *Missiologie* I (Brussels, Louvain and
Paris, 1939): 86–87. This passage is quoted by Yves de
Montcheuil in *Aspects de l'Eglise* (Paris: Cerf, 1949), 23.

tian school of Alexandria. He discusses the spiritual vision which, piercing through appearances, sees everywhere in the visible world a symbol of that which is invisible. But this is something altogether different from what Fr. Schillebeeckx has in mind when he considers the relationships between the Church and the world; it is a question of something that he calls (in a derogatory sense, which from his point of view may be justified, but which he does not analyze closely enough), the "theophanic world of former times". For him, not for Newman, this is the world that modern science and "the new experience of existence" have caused to vanish by "ridding religion and the Church of those elements which sacralizing religion had appropriated, and had, by that fact, withdrawn from their original worldly profane condition".[48]

V

"A theophanic world"; "sacralizing religion"; the notion of a "stopgap God"; if Fr. Schillebeeckx does not indeed consider these expressions as entirely equivalent, he associates them with each

[48] Schillebeeckx, *Approches théologiques*, vol. 3, 136–37. On the other hand, a collective work in four volumes was edited by Herder (Freiburg-im-Brisgau) under the title *Sacramentum Mundi: theologisches Lexicon für die Praxis* (1968–1969).

other and treats them as it were *per modum unius*, as expressing beliefs and mental attitudes which have gone out of style and need to be condemned and which the Church owes it to herself not only to correct but to reject in order to return the "world" fully to its "worldly state". Less radical than other thinkers, he does not reject "the religious" or "religion", but like many others he has nevertheless, or perhaps he had at one time, a horror for "the sacred", for "sacrality", any kind of sacrality. For him this term is always a certain indication of paganism, ignorance or superstition. He imagines, in fact, that a "sacred" world, or a world in which the "sacred" exists, is always an illusory world because it is considered, in part or entirely, as "divine". Since the biblical revelation made this false divinity of the world disappear, there cannot be, except as a pernicious remnant, anything truly "sacred" in the Bible, especially in the New Testament.[49] Showing itself less categorical and much wiser, Vatican II certainly did not intend to make any concession to paganism (or to show disdain for modern science) when it spoke of the sacrifice of the Mass or the sacrifice of the Cross, when it extolled the "original dignity and the

---

[49] This is an *a priori* decision which the least unbiased reading would lead one to question.

privileged and sacred value of the married state" or when it declared marriage to be "a sacred bond".[50]

As we see it, our author has once again allowed himself to be entangled in a false dilemma. This, fortunately, did not prevent him from mentioning (this time in perfect agreement with Vatican II, down to the very terms used) "the sacrament of episcopal consecration".[51] This is all the more interesting since many writers today, scrupulously eager to follow to the letter the Council's documents which they have not read very attentively, no longer dare to express themselves in that way.[52] Nor does our author hesitate to say, as we have repeatedly noticed, that the Church is a sacrament.

[50] *Gaudium et spes*, no. 47, 3 and no. 48, 1.

[51] Schillebeeckx, *L'Eglise du Christ*, 101. Cf. *Lumen Gentium*, no. 21: "*In episcopali consecratione. . . . Docet autem Sancta Synodus episcopali consecratione plenitudinem conferri sacramenti ordinis.*" In *Christus Dominus*, no. 3: "*Hoc suum episcopale munus, quod per consecrationem episcopalem susceperunt. . .*"; no. 4: "*Episcopi, vi sacramentalis consecrationis. . . .*" See Philips, *L'Eglise et son mystère*, vol. 1, 254, 259, 263, 273.

[52] Ever since this expression was in some sort canonized by an Ecumenical Council, it is noticeable, at least in France, that its use has been generally banished. This is a minor, innocent, very harmless indication, among other more serious ones, that it is not always the actual teaching of the Council which seems to guide the "postconciliar Church".

But it would be difficult to rob these words of all sacred connotations. Again, he does not fear to speak of "the *ecclesial*, sacred and special expression of the theological life of believers".[53] But when it comes to the world, his demand for strict purity prevails. As we have seen, the only adjective proper to qualify the world is "holy". It is "*holy ground*". It has been holy from the beginning, since it was "created in Christ". This, at least, is one of the explanations of that apparently strange formula which we called attention to earlier: "the world is implicit Christianity". These words do not presuppose that any human gaze was allowed to dwell on the reality of this "world" nor on the course of its history; no attention is paid to any contribution made by Christianity which might have had some influence in the field of conscience, of sentiments, of morals, of legislation, etc. This customary lack of interest in actual history, joined to an honorable fear lest the Church should congratulate herself on these benefits and begin singing her own praises, all this seems to us to be a large part of the myth of "implicit Christianity", thus generalized—but which we nevertheless do not confuse with a universal state of grace.

To guard against false interpretations the author

[53] Schillebeeckx, *Approches théologiques*, vol. 3, 155.

has taken pains to show that he does not claim as "implicit Christians" all those who were not, or are not, in the Church, any more than one can declare all the explicit Christians (ecclesial Christians) to be "authentic Christians". For him, "implicit Christianity" is a state, a "situation" which "may be accompanied by a refusal of grace".[54] He goes on to state, in addition and much to the point, "we are certainly aware of the ambivalence of human liberty, its capacity to choose good or evil. But our confidence in God is greater than the ambivalence of human liberty."[55] On that point, of course, we certainly agree with him.

Yet, we are told again in *Eglise et monde*[56]— and this is something rather different—that "in the present economy of salvation, where the Incarnation *took place*, the 'world' is *implicit Christianity*; it is an adequate, not sacred, but *sanctified* expression of man's communion with the living God".[57] So, it is no longer declared holy ever since its creation; it has been sanctified by the Incarnation. In a more

[54] Ibid., 155, note, and 157.
[55] Ibid., 182, note. Cf. "L'Eglise et l'humanité", 72.
[56] Schillebeeckx, *Approches théologiques*, vol. 3, 155.
[57] Italics added on "has taken place" and "sanctified". The Church is the "*sacred* expression, instituted in a particular way", of this communion: ibid.

precise manner, and one even less compatible with the expressions cited earlier, we are also told in a somewhat later text that "wherever Christianity appears the movement of desacralizing secularization is set in motion and the *sanctification* of the world begins." The two processes move ahead side by side, so closely linked together that one might at first believe that they are actually one, like the two sides of a single reality.[58] Still, here and there, a different point of view comes to the fore, inviting us to gaze beyond this struggle between the "sacred" and the "holy". Sanctification is never fully achieved; it always faces opposition, for "the history that is leading the world towards its consummation is traversed by two great currents: that of good . . . and that of evil. . . . Wherever the Kingdom of God moves in, Satan arises to combat it. . . . The history of the world . . . is drawing to a close, towards the Antichrist as well as towards the Lord's Parousia."[59]

[58] Cf. "La Vie religieuse dans un monde sécularisé", 283. Just as was common three years earlier, we frequently come across terms like "the worldly world", "nondivine", "given back to its worldliness", "intramundane reality", "profaneness", "profane objectivization", etc.

[59] Schillebeeckx, "Le 'Surnaturalisme': les espoirs chrétiens et non chrétiens concernant l'avenir", article in Dutch published in 1959; French trans. in *Approches théologiques*, vol. 3, 215.

This time we are fully in touch with reality, and in their general meaning these last sentences agree in advance and fully with *Gaudium et spes*.[60] We are authorized to think that there is no real contradiction here to the affirmations which later prevailed. Quite simply, the author was not able to avoid the multiple meanings contained in the ambiguous word "world". No more than those whom he reproached was he able to spare his reader possible misunderstandings by clearly explaining this plurality of meanings.[61]

But now we come to what seems to be a third meaning, when we read, in 1967, that the Christian, who can "*never* come to terms with the established order of things", "must change the world"; and for this he must "take sides with the 'revolutions' provoked more or less all over the world out of concern for man".[62] We are called upon to "speak clearly of the concrete means offered to us for building the world of the future: the Marxist

[60] Cf. *Gaudium et spes*, no. 9, 4, and no. 37, 2–3.

[61] Still, some brief references to "the biblical vision of the cosmos" had been given in 1951 in "Religion et monde", *Approches théologiques*, vol. 3, 67–71.

[62] Schillebeeckx, "Foi chrétienne et attentes terrestres", Dutch text 1967; French trans. in *Approches théologiques*, vol. 4, 67–71. Cf. "Le Christianisme implicite, domaine du Schéma 13", ibid., 47–48.

hope".[63] This would be, "at least in one sense", according to a text dating back to 1963, the essential request made by the Constitution *Gaudium et spes* which endorsed the "breakthrough" made by "new theological orientations" and canonized "the beginning of a new life for the Church"—all initiatives to which we owe a "rediscovery of the Gospel".[64]

VI

Still, does this really amount to a third meaning? Was this not already implied in the second one? Are the sanctification of the world already created by God and the technical construction of a new politico-social world really proposed to us as two truly distinct realities that in the last analysis belong to different orders? Perhaps. All this might be nothing more than a question of over-hasty

[63] Ibid., 75.

[64] H. Hillenaar and K. Peters, eds., *Les Catholiques hollandais, rencontres et dialogues*, French trans. J. Alzin (Brussels and Paris: DDB, 1963), x and 9. In fact, if the Council "exhorts Christians . . . to carry out their earthly tasks with zeal and fidelity, while letting themselves be guided by the spirit of the Gospel" (*Gaudium et spes*, 43, 1), it is far from obliging them to embrace these "terrestrial expectations", something which was being suggested to it in advance.

analyses or simple oversight.[65] But the context makes it doubtful. In fact, "to make oneself at home in the established order" would "by definition be to renounce eschatological hope". Between the "development of the world" and entry "into the new heaven and the new earth", nothing shows us that there is not simply a maturation but a real discontinuity, a radical break, and that this objective construction of a new society and the secret flowering of the Kingdom do not proceed in step with each other. "The building up of temporal society . . . brings into being an implicit Christianity"—not, perhaps, if we consider it in the abstract, but at least because one must always suppose that it "is concretely introduced into the absolute and gratuitous proximity of the mystery of grace".[66] But what is the basis for such an assurance presented as an obligation? "In humanity's struggle for a better world the

[65] This might have been suggested by some hints thrown out in 1965, though these were not too clear: "In the Church of Christ we find two distinct dialectical aspects: the Church as a community of life guided by the Spirit and active in the apostolic ministry of her worldwide apostolate, and the Church guided by the same Spirit but acting in the individual consciences of Christians": "L'Eglise et l'humanité", in *Approches théologiques*, vol. 3, 183. We find the same text, with slight differences in translation, in *Dogmatique*, 73.

[66] Schillebeeckx, *Approches théologiques*, vol. 3, 159.

Church must first of all discover the deep intention (perhaps unconscious) which reaches far beyond the inner-worldly sphere."[67]

Are we not, in this way, being invited to abdicate our critical faculty,[68] both as regards the objective value of the socio-political projects which we are asked to embrace and as regards the "intentions" of their promoters? We are told, in fact, as though to rob us of any excuse, that the struggle "for a better world" (but what kind of better world? and by what means?) "has no meaning without an implicit faith in the absolute salvation of the person, even though this might be denied on the level of an explicit ideology".[69] But whether one admits these views or not, must we in practice always, under pain of being unfaithful to the Gospel, consent in advance to be the dupes of all "the drumbeats for liberty in justice and love"?[70]

---

[67] Ibid., 158.

[68] However, commenting on the ideas of Harvey Cox (in *God's Revolution and Man's Responsibility*, 1965), who wrote, "at the present time, is God not present above all in the Marxist and Freudian revolution?", Schillebeeckx finds that this betrays a "unilateral character", as does the entire theology of "the death of God" school: "Foi chrétienne et attentes terrestres", 67–68.

[69] Schillebeeckx, "L'Eglise et le monde", in *Approches théologiques*, vol. 3, 158.

[70] Cf. Gaston Fessard, *Chrétiens marxistes* (Namur and Paris: Lethielleux, 1978), 389.

Finally, to win our definite agreement, we are reminded that "the important thing is not to cry out at the top of our voices that charity is everything in life but to know how to stop along the road to bring effective help to others."[71] An excellent consideration, like many others found in these articles of *Approches*, even though one might well reply that this call to action is not in fact the act itself. But we do not see how this Gospel truism makes it obligatory for us to adopt "the new theological orientations" that have been laid before us.

Be that as it may, does the "eschatological kingdom" not appear, in all this, as the culmination of our "earthly expectations", as their supreme fulfillment and consummation? Once again, this is how one should understand "the mysterious link" that *Gaudium et spes* forges between them in "one of its most fundamental insights".[72] So, in practice, human history and salvation history would be one and the same. "In this respect there is no difference between the Old and the New Testament."[73] Consequently, "today's Christian reflection" eliminates "the ancient problem of nature-supernature", traces of which, in the early days of the Council, could still be found in the first drafts of what was

[71] Schillebeeckx, "L'Eglise et le monde", 159.
[72] Schillebeeckx, "Foi chrétienne et attentes terrestres", 67.
[73] Cf. Schillebeeckx, "Le 'Surnaturalisme' ", 210.

then called Schema 17.[74] "Creation and divinization together make up the unique supernatural order of salvation."[75]

Considered in God's design it is certainly clear that all duality vanishes. Nor would we find any difficulty in granting that a certain rather modern discussion of "nature-supernature" ("in the medieval sense" or the "Neoscholastic sense") did not deserve to be perpetuated. Finally, in a wide sense we willingly admit that all of human history might be included in the term "salvation history"—provided that Christ's definitive saving act is not attenuated or left out of consideration.[76] When we are told for instance that the history of every man "is carried on in Christ" and that "in

[74] Schillebeeckx, "Foi chrétienne et attentes terrestres", 49 and 75. This is found again in the collection *Commentaire sur Gaudium et spes* (Paris and Tours: Mame, 1967), 149–50.

[75] Schillebeeckx, "Le Peuple de Dieu et le ministère ecclésial" (1949), in *Approches théologiques*, vol. 4, 88.

[76] Cf. *Dei Verbum*, chap. 1: *"Opus salutare consummat"*. See the collection of essays entitled *Mysterium Salutis*, French trans. (Paris: Cerf, 1969), vol. 1, and my commentary on the first chapter of *Dei Verbum* (*La Révélation divine*, Unam Sanctam 70 [Paris: Cerf, 1968], vol. 1): on the notion of salvation history, 184–96; on the stages and the conclusion of this history, 197–240. "The history of salvation", as Karl Barth so rightly remarked, "can never be inscribed on a table of synchronic history": *La Théologie protestante au XIXe siècle*, trans. L. Jeanneret (Geneva, 1969), 325.

him this history becomes salvation history",[77] no misunderstanding is possible. The unique role of Christ is given its due importance and one can easily see that every man needs to make his own the salvation won once for all by Christ's redeeming act. One can also see that "there is a difference between the time that ran from Abraham to Moses and that which extends from the Annunciation to the Parousia."[78] Our author himself had explained this very well in 1959. Before Christ,

> the ultimate meaning of human existence remained entirely open. . . . In Christ, God gave it definitive expression. This statement is presented to us as a definitive reality . . . "I have conquered the world." The victory is an accomplished fact, irrevocable. . . . Christ is the ἔσχατον . . . the Lord is the "new creation" and, in his humanity, the ἔσχατον is already an achieved reality.[79]

It could not be better put. However, in what is presented to us afterwards as a paraphrase of *Gaudium et spes*, we find it difficult to adopt

[77] Cf. John Paul II at Warsaw, June 1979.
[78] J.-R. Armogathe, "Pour une histoire sainte de l'Eglise", in *Communio* 6 (Nov.–Dec., 1979): 4.
[79] Schillebeeckx, "Le 'Surnaturalisme' ", 211–14.

indiscriminately the various blockings suggested to us. Just as we did not find in *Lumen Gentium* a "Church which is the sacrament of the world", we do not now find in *Gaudium et spes* the "mysterious link" of parallel growth as it is explained to us. If the Constitution does indeed oblige us, as Fr. M.-D. Chenu rightly says, to ask ourselves "how the Christian should coordinate his participation in the construction of the world and his communion in the divine life in Christ's Kingdom",[80] it certainly does not invite us to confuse the progress or the "construction" of the world with the new creation or even to suppose that the latter is an outgrowth of the former. The terms that the Council document offers us are carefully balanced. If we are told that "earthly progress" is "very important for the Kingdom of God", it still must be "carefully distinguished from the growth of Christ's reign"; or else we must come to an understanding about the meaning of this equivocal word "progress". If the Kingdom of God is "already present on this earth", it is so "mysteriously", namely in the depths of men's hearts, in that holiness which the Church must promote through the fruits of the Spirit who dwells in her and

[80] M.-D. Chenu, *La Théologie du renouveau* (Montreal, Paris and Toronto, 1968), vol. 1, 25.

through the external, observable results, measurable in human terms, of the progress of society. *His in terris Regnum jam in mysterio adest.*[81] "It will attain its perfection" and will be manifested for all to see "when the Lord returns".[82] These distinctions are all the more remarkable since the theme of this "chapter in *Gaudium et spes*" is the contribution offered by the Church to the earthly progress of society.

Lumen Gentium had already taught the same thing. *Gaudium et spes*, when beginning to explain the mutual relationships between the Church and the world, declares that "we suppose that all the teaching already given by the Council on the mystery of the Church has been accepted."[83] It would be good to reread this passage which, too often quoted partially, may have led some to conclude that this world itself was "God's eschatological city": "The final age of the world has already come upon us. The renovation of the world has been irrevocably obtained and in this

[81] Cf. Mk 1:15; Mt 4:17; Lk 10:10; 17:20–21.

[82] *Gaudium et spes*, pt. 1, chap. 3, no. 39, 3. Cf. G. Martelet, "L'Eglise et le temporel", in *L'Eglise de Vatican II* (Paris: Cerf, 1966), vol. 2. In this connection, see my book *Athéisme et science de l'homme: une double requête de Gaudium et spes*, Foi vivante (Paris: Cerf, 1968), 113–30.

[83] *Gaudium et spes*, 40, 1.

age is already anticipated in all reality. For even now in this earth the Church is adorned with a genuine though imperfect holiness."[84]

No doubt, "until there is a new heaven and a new earth where justice dwells (2 Pet 3:13), she bears in her sacraments and institutions the figure of the age which is passing"; but, "enriched by the gifts of her Founder and faithfully keeping his precepts of charity, humility and abnegation, she receives the mission of announcing the Kingdom of Christ and of God and of establishing it among all nations, forming the seed and the beginning of this Kingdom on earth"; even though it may often "look like a small flock", she "nonetheless constitutes a lasting and sure seed of unity, hope and salvation for the whole human race".[85]

VII

Perhaps, once again, what is at stake in this debate is less an irreducible opposition of ideas than a diversity in points of view. Perhaps again the

[84] This teaching in no way excludes a possible participation of "anonymous" or "implicit" Christians in the establishment of the Kingdom.

[85] *Lumen Gentium*, chap. 2, no. 17, and nos. 5 and 9. It is especially on chapters 1, 2 and 7 of *Lumen Gentium* that *Gaudium et spes* is based.

argument might be reduced, at least in part, to a question of semantics. Perhaps there is nothing more in all this than a clash between two schools of thought, a clash which might finally be resolved in a converging viewpoint. In the last analysis, is it fitting to "finalize the Church by the world", or, on the contrary, to "finalize the world by the Church"? These are the terms in which Abbé Monchanin, an acute dialectician as well as a deeply spiritual man, summed up the final problem of salvation.[86] Was the world "created for the Church"? or was the Church instituted for the world?[87] We have here an opposition which seems fundamental and which it may be good, indeed in certain contexts necessary, to confront in all its radicalness. But it should tend to soften as the meanings of the two words change, as the distance between the two positions is reduced. Might this not be, at bottom, what Fr. Schillebeeckx would like to suggest when in a paradoxical manner he envisions a double process: one of *ecclesialization* in humanity in general and another of *sanctifying*

[86] Abbé Monchanin, *Ermites du Saccidananda* (Paris: Casterman, 1956), 22. See the context in my *Images de l'Abbé Monchanin* (Paris: Aubier-Montaigne, 1967), 110–11, and the indications given by me in *La Pensée religieuse du Père Teilhard de Chardin* (Paris: Aubier-Montaigne, 1962), 35–38.

[87] Cf. Robert Guelluy, *Vie de foi et tâches terrestres* (Desclée, 1960), 40.

secularization in the Church? At least, might we not understand the matter in this way? While remaining opposed, as we have seen, to some of the explanations offered to us, we should like to see a symbol of this desired convergence in an expression of Origen's quoted by our author: ὁ κόσμος τοῦ κοσμοῦ ἡ 'εκκλησία. ["The world of the world—the Church".—Ed.] Each of the two terms of this elliptic sentence can be taken in turn as the subject and as the attribute. "Outside of Christ, and thus outside of his body, there is no salvation; but we must recognize that here below the Church is not yet fully what she is to become. . . . The world of men, having finally attained the fullness of *order* (that is, of peace and of communion), is in reality the Church."[88]

This convergence is essential, but perhaps up to now it has been a dream more than an actuality; it is a convergence in which the discussion begun here might eventually be absorbed but within which an alternative still remains, depending on how one understands this "order" and this final "peace" which will prevail in the end. The relationship "between the earthly future and the eschatological expectation leaves the field open to two types of Christianity: the one concerned

---

[88] Schillebeeckx, "L'Eglise et l'humanité", 183 and 186.

above all with bearing witness to this eschatological expectation, the other striving to prepare in some manner the material for the final Kingdom by striving to construct a better earthly future."[89] Without forcing the alternatives any further, we should prefer to phrase them differently: What should we like to see looming ahead "on the horizon of the ultimate future" (Monchanin)? Where shall we place the most *intrinsic* anticipation of this coming era in which "God will be all in all"? Will the eschatological Jerusalem rise before our eyes as the fulfillment of a social order undergoing continual progress here below? Or will it be the revelation of a communion of saints which as yet is invisible to us? Must it be the consequence and the reign of an objectively impeccable "orthopraxis" or of the "charity" lauded by St. Paul—that charity without which "nothing is of any use"? Will its innermost substance, and consequently its most immediate preparation, be in our estimation (in the Christian sense of the words) action or contemplation? Since we must make use of symbols, should we imagine it as the eternal summit of a

[89] Schillebeeckx, "Foi chrétienne et attentes terrestres", 61. But also in *Le Christ sacrement de la rencontre de Dieu* (Paris: Cerf, 1960), 245: "The Church has not yet entered her final stage. . . . In heaven alone will the Church, even as an external institution of salvation, achieve her full stature."

temporal construction or as the "consummation of the divine milieu"? In short, if tomorrow as today "the glory of God" must be "man who lives", must this life be envisaged first of all after the fashion of some ideal terrestrial city, or should we not rather say, with St. Irenaeus, that "man's life is the vision of God"?

APPENDIX C

THE COUNCIL
AND THE PARA-COUNCIL

Just as the Second Vatican Council received from a number of theologians instructions about various points of the task it should assume, under pain of "disappointing the world", so too the "post-conciliar" Church was immediately and from all sides assailed with summons to get in step, not with what the Council had actually said, but with what it should have said.[1] The matter we discussed in the previous Appendix was only one particular and partial episode, which we need not blow up out of proportion, in a much more general and vast phenomenon which, all polemics aside, deserves to be kept in mind in its various manifestations, examined in its sources and analyzed in its effects

[1] The Ultramontanes in 1870 had done the same for Vatican I and continued to do so for a long time; but they too were far from successful in their efforts.

by the historians of the contemporary Church. This is the phenomenon which we should like to designate as the "para-Council".[2]

Faithful to the promptings given by John XXIII, the Council wanted to bring about an *aggiornamento* needed by the Church if she were to renew herself; and it can be said that despite some tenacious opposition this purpose was achieved. More truly traditional than some of its opponents, the Council cleared the way which the Church must pursue in order to remain faithful to the mission received from her Lord. What the para-Council and its main activists wanted and demanded was a *mutation*: a difference not of degree but of nature.[3] The question was not whether progress should be slower or quicker, whether some halts were needed between stages, whether the goal envisaged should be nearer at hand or further away, whether, in the same spirit of fidelity, more

[2] This word has also sometimes been used to designate what went on in Rome itself during the Council. This has been described in the chronicles of René Laurentin, who speaks of "the conciliar and paraconciliar activity" or "the activity at the periphery of the Council": *Bilan du concile* (Paris: Seuil, 1966), 52–53. We do not use the term in this episodic and limited sense but, as the reader will perceive, in a wider and more specifically doctrinal sense.

[3] "Aggiornamento ou mutation?" is the title of a pamphlet that came out in 1965, but which it is too early to discuss.

boldness or more caution would be preferable. The objectives sought by the two sides were not the same.

Which of the two, the Council or the para-Council, has succeeded best? The question is too broad, too ambitious and too premature for us to feel tempted to furnish an answer here. No doubt, faith alone makes us certain that in the long run the Council will prevail—and this does not prevent us from perceiving some of its good effects every day. But which of the two received more attention from public opinion? Which has most often inspired those "prophetic" undertakings which led nowhere, those hyperbolic eulogies, those programs that announced Year One of the true Christianity that had been betrayed for the past twenty centuries? Which one, even today, is extolled more highly, is better served by the publicists who are most highly regarded and are in the best positions to make themselves heard and to impose their point of view?[4] Events make it necessary to ask these questions; and perhaps they make the answer no less inevitable. In any case, one thing seems

[4] "For two thousand years", we read the other day in a work by one of those publicists acting as a spiritual leader, "the message of Jesus has been travestied." Of course he put himself forward with his own formula and a lot of fancy verbiage.

beyond question: among many people, whether partisans or opponents or simply docile followers (all of whom were equally fooled), this para-Council, which often deserved the name of "anti-Council", has been mistaken for the true Council; and whatever in the latter's work did not correspond with the former's program has more than once been neglected or misrepresented.

From among certain intellectuals whose faith was not very enlightened, who lacked real culture and were ignorant of history and who were already more or less led astray by the millenarian delusions of our century, the pseudoconciliar ideology, allied as it was with a considerable portion of the press, recruited many partisans. We shall give only one example of this because it belongs to yesterday and because in a few pages it gathers together, in their most general terms, several characteristic themes of this ideology. We are speaking of a pamphlet, published with praiseworthy intentions; and while its author liked to think of himself as audacious, he did not wish to be considered subversive. Indeed, the publication might even be considered as specially "authorized".

"If the Church herself", we read in this pamphlet, "did not take part in the great mutation of the world, she would no doubt be forever disqualified."

So what we need is "a Church undergoing rapid mutations", a Church whose "entire content of faith" must be "reinterpreted in terms of the new problems which the world faces", a Church that can no longer be defined "according to a descending schema", but according to "an ascending schema". She will no longer have to transmit a heritage, for henceforth she will "be based less on fidelity to a tradition than on a future that must be invented". She will no longer be "a Church laying down eternal verities" but "a locus for creativity, invention, newness". She will no longer need to "defend the deposit of faith" but must rather adapt herself humbly to "the new art of living" which the world is in the process of beginning. Of course, she will not claim to possess anything "sacred" or to consider herself "the guarantor of the religious". "Urged on by the Spirit", she will have left behind "her old crumbling walls" to build for herself "humble, functional houses, indwelt by love . . . which will be the homes of liberty, where something new and great will take place". In fact, "we do not know what she will be, but we must aid in bringing her to birth. . . ."

"In fact", this idyllic dream, floating about in the ether, if it ever became a reality as it claims it wants to do, might well turn out to be the flowery garden through which we would be led, as so often happens, into an arbitrary "structure", constraining in a different fashion than those structures we knew in the Church of old. The people who produce this kind of prose, made up from end to end of historico-Manichaean slogans, certainly do not see where they are being led and where they risk leading others. One would, of course, be mistaken if one attributed too much importance to many semantic excesses, due either to early enthusiasm for the work of the Council or more simply to the pomposity characteristic of journalism. When we read every day that "a new Church must be planted" or that "today we must start constructing a new Church", and so on, or when on the slightest pretext we hear of the "Copernican revolution" taking place in the Church, we do not always need to become alarmed. In addition, occasional furtive indications which escape the pens of some of these audacious neophytes are sometimes enough to reassure us as to their profound innocence.[5] Still, is it not usually with the wholesale complicity of the innocents, in troubled periods, that the worst deformations come about?

Without questioning the perfect sincerity of

[5] "The introduction of the method of human sciences into biblical study has shown us . . . that the Bible is not a book written at a single sitting."(!)

their convictions, it would still be insulting to treat the principal authors or promoters of the para-Council as merely "innocents". The instruments of their thinking are more subtle, more "sophisticated"; and they know the precise purposes for which they are using them. Certainly, some points in their program imposed in the name of "modernity" were softened quickly enough or were found to be less urgent than they were supposed to be. Thus, the "return of the sacred", however one may understand or evaluate that phenomenon, has inspired some doubts and even caused some changes of opinion in more than one uncompromising protagonist of "profaneness". Thus, again, as a result of causes which are only too well known, "Marxist hope" has undergone a loss of prestige—even though it still wins over a lot of dupes. But all these, as we say today, are only "incidents along the road". On the other hand, it is impossible that in the long run some exacting minds should not perceive the contradiction between what is proposed to them and the actual teaching of Vatican II. But then two or three very simple procedures, taken for methodological principles, make it possible for the apostles of the para-Council to regain their advantage.

The first procedure calls for a certain expertise combined with real attention to the texts. It consists in trying to find in the Council documents, every time that they do not conform with the desired program, traces of internal contradictions, with a view to demolishing their balance in favor of a unilateral thesis. Every effort towards a synthesis—an effort which is necessary everywhere for a correct exposition of Catholic truth, even if it does not always lead to a perfect result—is denounced as a merely political compromise; and the mechanism underlying it must be exposed so as to get down to the Council's "true" meaning. A minute (or supposedly such) investigation of the debates, of the amendments proposed and of the successive drafts can be very helpful here, on the condition that one has decided in advance what this "true meaning" should have been. "Today it may be regretted", writes a theologian whose euphemisms deceive nobody, "that the Council did not succeed in proposing a more coherent formulation of the majority consensus which one can read between the lines." He is talking about the second chapter of *Dei Verbum* on "the transmission of divine revelation". A similar remark had been made about the first chapter, on "revelation itself", by the advocates of a so-called existential faith which would not include any determination, any conceptual objectivation.[6] But how does one

---

[6] See my commentary on chapter 1 of *Dei Verbum* in the

discern this "majority consensus", supposing that it ever really existed?[7] And if by chance one did discern it, in the name of what principles would one prefer it to the definitive consensus expressed by the morally unanimous vote of the Fathers? Even if one considers these questions from a purely human standpoint, why could not a deeper study have been made to enlighten the Fathers on doubtful points that had passed unnoticed in projects which had not yet been sufficiently thought out? Is this not what happens to all of us? And why could the "majority" never have been enlightened on any point by a "minority" or even by a single member? Finally, why represent

first of the two volumes devoted to this Constitution (*La Révélation divine*, Unam Sanctam 70 [Paris: Cerf, 1968]), 161–302. On this capital point, in a passage dating back to 1958 which constitutes as it were an anticipated commentary on no. 5 of *Dei Verbum*, Fr. Schillebecckx had seen things more clearly: "In Holy Scripture the *fides fiducialis* is always accompanied by a profession of faith. In other words, the personal, existential act of faith, as a fundamental choice, can never be separated from 'dogmatic faith' in which one's personal option is entirely governed by the salvific reality which is presented. . . ." In *Approches théologiques*, trans. P. Bourgy (Brussels and Paris: Editions du C. E. P., 1965), vol. 1, 184; cited in my commentary, *La Révélation divine*, 252.

[7] Especially in the last case mentioned here, to suppose that some artificial compromise was accepted by the majority is pure imagination. See my commentary, with the historical indications, quoted in the previous note.

everything as a struggle between embattled parties? Anyone who saw at first hand how the Council "operated" and followed step by step the elaboration of the texts themselves can never be taken in by such phantasmagorical notions. We know, of course, that there were discussions, sometimes lively ones, and misunderstandings which needed to be cleared up (for instance, on the meaning of the word "college" in the Church's tradition, a meaning that seems entirely forgotten today by most of those who discourse on the subject). But a properly informed person would have a wholly different idea about the Council's work and its results from that of certain commentators who are too prone to "read between the lines". And he would be quite certain that a "majority" favoring a program even very approximately like that of some of the protagonists of the para-Council is a pure myth. This is something that the main players in this game know better than anyone else.

When Vatican II, in *Dei Verbum* (to mention it again), reminds us in complete agreement with Trent that the sole source of Christian revelation is the Gospel and when it specifies, further, that this Gospel "shines forth for us in Christ, who is at once its mediator and its plenitude", several writers pretend to understand that in saying this it had revised Trent by admitting Scripture alone as

the sole source and by leaving out Tradition—
something which is as contrary as possible to the
letter and to the spirit of the Constitution. By the
same kind of surgical treatment they drew from
Lumen Gentium, despite the evidence, a "Church-
communion" without any firm structures,[8] a
"collegiality" never heard of before,[9] a brand new
"people of God", a "non-sacerdotal ministry"
with a reduced or confused "specificity", etc. A
variant of the same procedure consists in opposing
one document to another so as to choose the one
that, because of its more particularized point of
view or its special terminology, best enables one
to sidestep a doctrinal teaching which is more
strongly stressed in the other. In short, remarks a
theologian quoted above: "in the last ten years
Catholic theology" (note this self-definition, this
canonization of a group which is expert in public
relations) "has been trying to resolve the ambiguities in Vatican II." It has been going at this task
with zest, urged on, in addition, by the "spirit of
the age" which makes people mistake this game of

[8] As early as 1967 Philips wrote, "The artificial antithesis
between a juridical Church and a community of love has
caused a great deal of mischief": *L'Eglise et son mystère au 2e
concile du Vatican* (Desclée, 1967), vol. 1, 274.

[9] See Philips' commentary on the Council's text: ibid.,
272–316.

dichotomies, this hunt for antitheses, for the perfection of the critical spirit.[10]

The second procedure, which also includes variations, is even simpler. It does not "fiddle" with the texts. It consists in stating frankly in a given case (and these cases, which may be rather numerous, often concern some of the Council's major texts) the reasons why one should not pay any attention to them.

The Council Fathers, we are told, carried out, and could only carry out, a very imperfect task. Old habits of thought could not be dropped overnight, and these "did not allow the intuitions of Vatican II to produce their effects". So the new doctrine, which was supposedly that which in the depths of their hearts the Fathers really wanted to promote, "did not succeed in finding expression in the official documents". In a word, the Council "was paralyzed by old-fashioned aims". These "aims", consciously entertained, inhibited these

[10] A certain school of exegesis had been practicing this for a long time on certain biblical passages, performing dissections in the name of a logic of thought that considered itself trenchant and was merely narrow. In a single epistle of St. Paul, for instance, or in the entire Pauline *corpus*, it was claimed that the so-called "mystical" passages and the "eschatological" passages could not possibly have been written by the same author.

"intuitions" (subconscious? unconscious?), and it was the former which were enshrined in the documents themselves. In their turn, alas, the popes, too, remained faithful to these "aims" and by that fact they proved unfaithful to the "intuitions of Vatican II". So it is up to us, the theologians, aware as we are of the needs of the hour and impelled by the winds of history, to discover and to proclaim the doctrine which the Council secretly wished to state without having succeeded in doing so.

There is a slightly different explanation which is less subtle. If the work of the Council is indeed very imperfect, its authors, we are told, were quite aware of it; what paralyzed them was nothing but timidity. They did not dare carry their "intuitions" to their logical conclusions. But after remaining stationary for so long, how could such a prodigious leap be made! The Christian people would not have followed it. No doubt, also, "those of the world's bishops who were not yet capable of following the movement would in practice have paralyzed the Council's decisions." So, one can disregard a certain number of "second-rate documents". Again, the world is moving ahead rapidly, so that what was acceptable in the 1960s is no longer so in the 1970s. But, we are further assured, the essential part of the Council's labors remains;

it authorized the most startling innovations, for this essential element is not found in the contents of the documents, in the letter, but is entirely contained in its orientation, its spirit. This was basically an "open" Council. "At the time of Vatican II", we are told in one instance, "the Church had a lot of catching up to do, and many things have continued to evolve since then, beginning with the situation of Christianity in our own countries. . . . The Council did not so much lay down a program of reforms that were not to be exceeded as it welcomed a new spirit of renewal with inexhaustible applications."

This last statement would be less open to objection if it were presented under a much less generalized guise. Clearly, in the different decrees of the Council, just as in those of preceding Councils (beginning with the "Council" of Jerusalem), one can find certain purely disciplinary decisions which do not claim to be eternal. There are also judgments and directives applying to certain concrete situations. This is particularly the case as regards *Gaudium et spes*, which is entitled "Pastoral Constitution on the Church in the Modern World", and more especially the case for its second part which deals with "various more urgent problems". It offers several practical considerations which some day will be (and in fact some may already be)

out-of-date, at least when taken literally. The
Fathers of the Council were not unaware of this
inevitable caducity as we can see by this remark at
the close of *Gaudium et spes*: "Since we have been
dealing here with topics which are in constant
evolution, the teaching presented here . . . must
be further pursued and amplified" (no. 91, 2).
That was why a number of the Fathers would have
preferred that several chapters of this second part
should be treated in an encyclical, or relegated to
an appendix, with annexed documents. After
much hesitation,[11] the opposite opinion, which
had good arguments in its favor, prevailed.[12] But
the authors who invoke, without real discernment,
the "intuitions" of the Council as an excuse for
disregarding the letter of the documents themselves, seem to forget three things:

1. Not all the work of the Council, far from it,

[11] Cf. the account of some of these incidents in J. Y.
Calvez, "La Communauté politique", in *L'Eglise dans le monde
de ce temps, Gaudium et spes, commentaires du Schéma XIII* (Paris
and Tours: Mame, 1967), vol. 2, 289; also R. Tucci, "Historique de la constitution", ibid., 86–87, 101, 104, 112.

[12] Cf. the sensible remarks made by one of the lay obser-
vers at the Council, the Anglican John Laurence (ibid., 400):
"Many things in the second part of Schema 13 will soon be
out-of-date, but that will be a reminder that they must
continually be revised and perfected. This does not apply to
the first part of the Schema. . . ."

consisted in laying down "a program of reforms" liable to be exceeded or not. The Council reminded us at length, sometimes under a different form, often with additional precise details or by insisting on certain aspects that time had more or less obscured, of many essential points of doctrine and discipline and of the Church's tradition that it consolidated. Even if the remainder of these points should give rise to many reforms, they themselves do not fall under the law of time. It is not legitimate to invoke that law to set aside the teachings of the Church on the eucharistic mystery, for instance, or on the ministerial priesthood. Otherwise, this kind of "progress", without guidelines and consequently without clear directions, would end in dissolution and ruin. This would not be a fruitful, because "homogeneous", evolution, as the great Newman said, but mere change based on the various "models" offered us from day to day by shifting types of political societies, by current ideals of "modernity", by various tendencies to desacralization or secularism. One can judge, therefore, the value one should attach, depending on how it is understood, to the slogan which is so lightly invoked to the effect that the Council "was not a goal but a starting point".[13]

[13] We have come across the following variant of this principle, advanced as an axiom to justify this or that pro-

2. The "renewal" whose "spirit" is invoked is not necessarily what this or that individual, what a particular theologian with his individualistic notions or even that large, powerful group whose work of research was not equal either to its power of affirmation or to the publicity apparatus which it controlled might consider as such.

3. Finally, openly to contradict on this point or that the doctrinal teaching of the Council is surely not the best way to apply that teaching.[14]

Still, this famous "spirit of the Council", which those who invoke it most have nourished with their own ideologies, is so seductive and so powerful that it soon obliges its adorers to accept a whole "new theology", the foundation of a "new Church"; and if later on it happens that an unfortunate pope tries to show himself faithful to the truth that the Church has always believed in and that the Council itself once again stated, he finds

---

posed demolition: "Since Vatican II . . . we still have a long way to go." Another author, already quoted above, also speaks lyrically of "the constant gush of creative interpretation" that is "the only possible fidelity" in spite of the "fear" which it inspires "in conciliar theologians".

[14] We do not, of course, wish to affirm that the composition of *Gaudium et spes*, or of any other Council document for that matter, is a perfect masterpiece. Such an assertion would be worse than an error, an absurdity.

himself accused by overbearing critics of making himself the "triumphalistic herald" and the "super-annuated champion" of "old-time theology". His predecessor had been praised by a certain theologian for having exhorted us to "enter in an enlightened manner into the spirit of the Council", but at the same time he was blamed for having recommended to us in the same sentence "a faithful application of the Council's directions". Indeed, the Council was something wonderful the day it opened, a magnificent inaugural spectacle; but as soon as it began to "make concrete decisions" the charm began to fade, the danger of a "certain rigidity" appeared, and its spirit was no longer free and pure. Under those conditions (so one extremist concludes, logically enough), in order to be truly faithful to the Council one must "begin all over from scratch", without "repeating" anything of what it said. There could be no more complete divorce between the letter and the spirit than this.

Is there anything more opposed to the Spirit of God, as found in the New Testament, any sadder spectacle, than the arrogance of this new breed of spiritualism which many of these manifestoes illustrate so grievously?

We are told by one writer that there is a "logic of conciliar dynamism" which demands that we abandon the "official security", referred to "with a sort of defensive instinct" and in spite of "praiseworthy basic intentions" in the encyclicals of Paul VI; it leads us to oppose this security by facing the "total risk, the risk of not knowing, which is a condition for creative life and continuing interpretations". Another invites us to march ahead fearlessly, allowing ourselves to be carried by "the wind of the Spirit" so as "to invent new ways of believing", etc.

If recourse to the "spirit" of the Council or to "the logic of conciliar dynamism" is still frequent,[15] another expression, a vivid metaphor, seems to have become the favorite recently (our time is a great consumer of slogans). Its interpretation, or rather its exploitation, offers infinite resources. Vatican II made a "breakthrough"; or, as others say, it made a "breach" through which we can make a breakthrough. Without being too choosy one may amalgamate the three fatidical phrases: through the breach which the Council opened for us we are making a breakthrough, impelled by the breath of the Spirit. Now we can really feel at ease. We were prisoners; henceforth we are free. The Spirit has delivered us from the Institution.

[15] As we have seen, they also speak of "the intuitions". But these words can also be found in the works of excellent authors who respect the letter of the Council's decrees.

Each of these three expressions which we hear re-echoing around us has, we admit, a legitimate meaning. It is very true that the letter never suffices without the spirit. It is no less true that the Council did open a breach; and even though such military metaphors are hardly proper here, one can agree that this breach invites a breakthrough. But the spirit does not exist either without the letter; the breach is not opened so that we can throw all the contents into the street; and our breakthrough must not be made in order for us to leave our Mother and go and die of hunger and thirst in the desert.

Words, like things, have their uses; they can also be abused.[16]

The practical consequences of the para-Council, the groundwork for which was laid long before 1960, are in large part responsible for many of the reactions which, mistaking their object, have occurred during the last fifteen years against what many thought came from the Council itself. The

[16] "One cannot . . . undertake to create a doctrine more faithful to the Council than the doctrine actually taught by the Council itself. . . . This obviously does not exclude progress or ulterior developments. But this progress and these developments cannot contradict what was stated in the documents themselves": J. Galot, S.J., "Réinventer le sacerdoce?", in *Esprit et vie* [*L'Ami du clergé*] (Nov. 29, 1979), 629.

evil could only be aggravated thereby. Still, one can hardly expect to find in all the faithful a degree of discernment which would require, in addition to a perspicacious intellect, the means of obtaining objectively valid information, a personal, attentive reading of the genuine texts, sometimes a critical evaluation of certain persons occupying important positions, etc. Confusion was, and in certain places still is, so deliberately fomented that it would be unjust to reproach many Catholics for being victimized by it. These people are not retarded, not instinctively hanging on to defensive positions; they simply want to remain faithful to the beliefs of the Church and have found themselves to a greater or lesser extent involved in inextricable contestations. In the same way, if many were infected by the spirit of agitation and the feverish pursuit of "novelties" during those same years, and did not know how to react, it was because they did not discern (and often enough really could not discern) either the tainted source of this propaganda in favor of "a new Church" or the destination to which it intended to lead them.

However, that the Council was not at the origin of a movement which tends to ruin the faith, and that it did not lend itself to such a result unwittingly by a series of imprecise and equivocal statements or tendentious omissions, is amply demonstrated by the texts themselves, the commentaries by those who were the main authors of the documents[17] and the teachings of the popes who ever since the Council have constantly referred back to the documents. This is no less true for *Gaudium et spes* (the only text that a number of people seem to want to understand—and this is to misunderstand it already[18]) than for all the others. Aware of the upheavals in our society, in which "the best and the worst" are mingled, and ready to hail all forms of progress which in their order can contribute to the rise of a better "humanism", Vatican II still rejected whatever might tend to reduce "man's integral vocation", his "journey to the heavenly

---

[17] Let us merely mention in particular the two volumes of Monsignor Gérard Philips, Vice-President of the Doctrinal Commission of the Council, who died prematurely as a consequence of the enormous amount of work he had done for that Commission: *L'Eglise et son mystère au 2ᵉ concile du Vatican: histoire, texte et commentaire de la constitution Lumen Gentium*.

[18] "If the aftermath of the Council has so often been disappointing, if it gave rise to uncontrolled and sometimes disastrous experiments, one may say that this was due to not having given to *Lumen Gentium* and to the two other constitutions that complete it (on the liturgy and on the word of God) the attention which they deserved": Cardinal Garonne, "*Lumen Gentium*, 15ᵉ anniversaire", in *L'Osservatore Romano*, French ed. (Nov. 27, 1979), 1–2.

city", and to close his mind to "the mystery of faith" (*Gaudium et spes*, nos. 56–57). When it stressed the autonomy of those areas which depend only on man's natural activity, it made clear the distinction between "nature" and the "supernatural", as well as their necessary union. Proposing to apply remedies to the "imbalance" which results from the accelerated "mutations" of our century, it tried to enlighten man regarding the mystery of his own being by presenting to him Jesus Christ, "the same yesterday, today and forever". (*Gaudium et spes*, nos. 5; 9; 10, 2, etc.)

For the para-Council, on the contrary, the Church, which has finally attained adulthood after an infancy that had lasted for twenty centuries, is bringing about "a radical revolution" within herself. She must no longer pretend to interpret the world to us in terms of the Christian faith; she must cease considering herself "as the depositary of the truth"! She must accept generalized "pluralism"; she must proceed to "secularize" herself; she must give herself a "democratic" structure, imitating that of modern states; she must cast aside those old wives tales about "interior life", and so on. Such were some of the fashionable slogans which, openly or in secret, wrapped in nebulous phraseology or not, had been circulating throughout the Western and Christian world ever more and more widely in the years before the Council. The Calvinist Karl Barth was a clear-sighted witness of all this, and the remarks he made about it in his great work, *Church Dogmatics*, transcend, as he himself said more than once, the frontiers of his own confession. The situation within the Catholic Church especially disturbed him.[19] "Inner secularization", he wrote in 1959,[20] "threatens the Church as such: her message, her doctrine, her order and her mission." Some people

> have found fault with what they call the sterile and static differentiation between the *ecclesia docens* and the *ecclesia audiens*; but in so doing they have come to question the fruitful, dynamic meaning of this differentiation; by stressing the non-holy priority of some human word they have questioned the holy priority of the Word of God, and they have managed to get rid of it more or less successfully. They talk of a "universal priesthood", under-standing by that expression the sovereignity of the individual or of the crowd. They thought they

[19] He repeated this to me with deep sorrow a short time before his death; he deplored the fact that certain priests had given up Marian devotion—a devotion which he himself did not practice, but he understood very well that nothing living would replace it in their souls.

[20] Karl Barth, *Dogmatique*, trans. Ryser (Geneva, 1972), vol. 4, bk. 3, 35–36. The original German edition came out in 1959.

were eliminating priests, theologians and preachers, but in reality they were turning away from the Lord of the whole Church. . . . While they explain and apply (and criticize too!) the Bible and dogma, while they rely on the Holy Spirit (who breathes where he wills) and on conscience to which each man is responsible, they have been able to bring out the notion of brotherhood in Christ, in theory; whereas in practice they have only succeeded in glorifying the ideas, the words and lives . . . of *homunculi* filled with covetous desires; and they sought to make these sovereign in the midst of the Church herself. On the other hand, if "ecclesiastics" and theologians have frequently shown themselves estranged from the "people", they have just as often proved to be entirely too soft and accommodating in their regard, quickly giving in to the latter's "desires", when what was involved would have demanded that they be vigilant, firm and sure guides. . . .

How many Christians with a very limited knowledge of ecclesiastical history give free rein, in dealing with tradition, to their limited common sense and their wandering imaginations; they gaily rush forward and simplify problems in their eagerness to show initiative. . . . [Their introduction into influential positions] opened wide the door to errors and confusions of the most varied sorts that threaten indeed not only an ancient "orthodoxy" or a more recent one but the very understanding of the Gospel itself and its progress. . . .

To these characteristics, noted by a Protestant some fifteen years ago, would we need to add a great many correctives so that the picture might apply to today's situation[21] in a portion of the Catholic Church (the proportions of which should not be exaggerated)? On the other hand, where, without preconceived convictions, would one find in the work of the Council the root of all this, or any sort of justification for it? One must rather admit that, under the influence of the para-Council, it is the capital points very expressly treated by the Council (especially as regards the Church herself) that are most often challenged today. "The evolution of the Church", wrote René Rémond, "has taken an entirely different direction from that which the Council expected and which the faithful also hoped for. Yet, for all that, I do not feel that I need to change my evaluation of the Council's work."[22] This, it seems to us, is also the sentiment of John Paul II.

[21] As late as 1968 Msgr. Philips, always so measured in his words, wrote (*L'Eglise et son mystère*, vol. 2, 345): "No one can close his eyes to the disorder that prevails in many places."

[22] René Rémond, *Vivre notre histoire* (Paris: Centurion, 1976), 125.

THE "CULT OF MAN": IN REPARATION TO PAUL VI

It is not without repugnance, indeed it is with a certain shame that we approach this topic. If it concerned only a passing episode, no matter how distasteful in itself, we would have let it slip into oblivion. But some fifteen years ago a public slur was made; from year to year it is repeated; it reverberates and falls on eager ears. . . . Recently it was taken up again in the most vehement and the most damning terms. If the truth is not finally and clearly established, this charge may pass on to posterity as something proved and settled. Now, this is not a question of censuring a discourse or a man. By the appraisal given to the work of Vatican II as presented by Paul VI, it amounts to a general judgment on the official attitude of the Catholic Church as a result of the Council. And this assessment, which is accepted as correct, is execrated by some, while for others it becomes a matter for praise, something that can give them comfort in the path of abandon in which they are walking and where they want us to walk with them.

I

At the final public session of Vatican II on December 7, 1965, Paul VI spoke, attempting to characterize the spirit which had guided the Council. Our times, he said, "are oriented more towards the conquest of the earthly than towards the heavenly Kingdom"; these are times when God is frequently forgotten, a forgetfulness which seems to be inspired by scientific progress; times when the human person, "who has come to a fuller realization of what he really is and what his liberty means, tends to affirm his absolute autonomy and to throw off the yoke of any law which transcends himself". Now, "it was in times such as these that the Council was held for the honor of God, in the name of Christ and under the guidance of the Holy Spirit." "Thanks to the Council", "the manner of conceiving man and the universe in reference to God as their center and their end has been set forth before humanity, with no fear of the accusation of being out-of-date and estranged from man." The world will "at first consider this view as foolish";

but the Church hopes that in the end the world will recognize it as "full of wisdom and a source of salvation". Still, since the Council "took very great interest in the study of modern man", it awakened in some people "the suspicion that an exaggerated tolerance and consideration for passing reality . . . had been embraced by some members of the Council and shown in some of its acts". Paul VI goes on to deny such a suspicion, stressing that "the rule followed at the Council was, above all, that of charity. And who can accuse it of having been wanting in religious spirit and in fidelity to the Gospel for having chosen this basic orientation, if one recalls that it was Christ himself who taught us to look upon love for our brethren as the distinctive sign of his disciples?"

Next there follows a telling sketch of man "as he is in our time", with his innumerable contradictions: "Man is entirely concerned about himself; he makes himself not only the center of all that interests him but even dares to claim that he is the principle and the final reason for all reality. . . . Man is caught up in tragedy, the victim of his own drama." When he wants to dominate others he becomes "selfish and cruel. . . . Man is not satisfied with himself . . . man is versatile . . . man is unbending . . . man thinks, loves, works, always expecting something: he is 'the child who

is growing' (Gen 49:22). Man is also sacred in
the innocence of his childhood, in the wretchedness of his poverty, in the agonizing sufferings he
endures. Man is a sinner, and man is a saint. . . ."[1]
We shall read the rest of the passage shortly; but
we already have the essential theme of the discourse, and its tone.

Some days later Abbé Georges de Nantes wrote:
"The discourse of J.-B. Montini promotes the
theses dear to Freemasonry."[2] Later, reiterating
his criticisms in a *Liber Accusationis*, he said, speaking of this same discourse: "Certainly there never
had been one like it in all the annals of the Church,
nor will there ever be another." To vindicate his
statements he quoted the passage which follows
immediately after the citation given above:

> A lay and profane humanism finally appeared, in
> all its monstrous mien, and in a sense it defied
> the Council. The religion of the God who made
> himself man confronted the religion—for it is
> truly such—of man who makes himself God.
>
> What happened? A confrontation? A battle? An
> anathema? This could have happened, but it did

[1] Abbé Georges de Nantes, in *Documentation catholique* 63
(1966): 61–62; French translation published by the Ufficio
Stampa and revised according to the Latin text.

[2] Quoted by Jean-François Six in *Le Courage de l'espérance:
les dix ans qui ont suivi le concile* (Paris: Seuil, 1978), 41.

not. The old story of the Samaritan inspired the Council's spirituality. Unbounded sympathy filled it entirely. The discovery of human needs (and they are all the more pressing in proportion as the son of earth[3] becomes greater) absorbed the attention of our Synod.

Give the Council credit for this, at least, you modern humanists who have denied the transcendence of supreme realities, and be willing to recognize our new humanism; we too, more than anyone, profess the cult of man.[4]

This passage provoked indignation against the author of such a speech "which ends by the proclamation, before all the world and before God, of the CULT OF MAN":

In the Gospel of Jesus Christ we are taught "to adore God alone and to serve him only" (Lk 4:8). We all know with what zeal the faithful were warned, during the Council and since its closing, not to exaggerate their devotion towards the Virgin Mary and the saints! And now, flatly violating the Gospel of Jesus Christ, we are given this "new humanism" of a Church which pro-

[3] Here the Abbé, who is quoting, inserted: (*sic*).

[4] Abbé Georges de Nantes, *Liber Accusationis in Paulum Sextum: Plainte pour hérésie, schisme et scandale au sujet de notre frère dans la foi, le pape Paul VI* (Saint Parres lès Vaudes, France. G. de Nantes, 1973), 19.

claims, by the mouth of the Pope and to the apparently unanimous acclamation of all the bishops of the world, that "more than anyone else, she professes the cult of man"![5]

II

This text calls for a number of remarks:

1. Let us note, first of all, that the author quotes nothing from the first part of the talk, which occupies four closely filled columns in *La Documentation catholique*, and which we summarized above. Of the paragraph that immediately precedes the passage exciting his ire, he quotes only one phrase, the one about man who "pretends to be the principle and the final norm of all reality". This completely falsifies the appraisal of man with his numberless contradictions sketched by Paul VI. Further, he disregards all the end of the talk, which occupies three more columns in *La Documentation catholique*, and in which the Pope shows that if the idea of serving man has occupied a central place at the Council, it did not "make the Church's thinking deviate in the direction of the anthropocentric positions adopted by modern

[5] Ibid. This passage was republished by Abbé de Nantes in his bulletin *La Contre-Réforme catholique au XXe siècle* 141 (May, 1979).

culture". "The Church", Paul VI added, "is concerned with man and with this world, but her inner impetus urges her on towards the Kingdom of God. . . . Is not man, left to himself, a mystery in his own eyes?" The Church explains man to himself, "in virtue of her own knowledge of God; to know man as he really is, the whole man, one must know God." Then the Pope quotes the burning words of St. Catherine of Siena: "It is in thy nature, O eternal God, that I shall know my own nature" (Or. 24). He goes on to say that "The Catholic religion is life because it . . . gives life its true meaning; it is life because it constitutes life's supreme law and infuses into it this mysterious energy which makes it, we can say, divine." The Council, in its love for man and its resolve to serve him, invites him to turn again through Christ to that God of whom St. Augustine could say: "To separate from him is to perish; to come back to him is to return to life; to remain in him is to be unshakeable; to seek him is to be reborn; to dwell in him is to live" (Sol. 1, 1, 3).

2. The author has read very distractedly the passage which he still does not fear to anathematize; or does he know so little of sacred Scripture, especially the Epistles of St. Paul whose name this Pope, with whom he grows so indignant, assumed? He did not perceive that in saying: "we

too, more than anyone, profess the cult of man",
Paul VI was inspired by the words of the Apostle
to the Corinthians: "Are they Hebrews? So am I.
Israelites? So am I. Descendants of Abraham? So
am I. Ministers of Christ? (I speak wild words!) So
am I, more than they" (2 Cor 11:22–23). No doubt
the situation is not exactly the same for both of
them. The Apostle was taking issue with "dis-
honest workmen that pass for apostles of Christ"
and "ministers of justice", like "Satan, who can
assume the guise of an angel of light" (2 Cor
11:13–15). But the trend of thought is the same,
and that *"more"*, that *a fortiori*, is at the same time,
in both cases, an opposition. Just as the first Paul
confronted one apostolate with another, one zeal
with another, so Paul VI is pitting one humanism
against another. To "the lay and profane humanism", the "religion of man who makes himself
God", he opposes the Church's humanism—
something he might have called her "integral
humanism"—the fruit of "the religion of the God
who became man". And what he does in this
passage is precisely what he had done from one
end of his discourse to the other.

3. He is doing it in no polemical spirit, but in
imitation of God, "the friend of man", in a burst
of sympathetic admiration for man, that marvel of
creation, made by the Creator in his own image

and for that reason exalted by the Bible and by the whole of Christian tradition—and at the same time in a sentiment of deepest pity for the calamities which overwhelm him. Immediately after the sentence where the Abbé of Nantes closes his quotation, the Pope is at pains to specify that the Council "took care to study man in the light of the divinity. It considered once again the eternal double visage of man: his wretchedness and his greatness, his profound, undeniable wound, incurable of itself, and the good which he still possesses, always bearing as he does the mark of hidden beauty and of unconquerable sovereignty." And while "denouncing the errors" of "today's human world", it still wished to show, "when addressing persons, nothing but consideration, respect and love". To all, it "addressed a pastoral and missionary invitation" drawn "from the light of the Gospel". From this flows a "decidedly optimistic attitude", which, the Pope hopes, will give its teachings "more attractiveness, vivacity and persuasive force".

4. Either the accuser of the Pope did not at all understand the texts that we have just mentioned and that are certainly in no way obscure; or he deliberately left them aside, although they formed the framework, one might say, of the whole discourse, and allowed himself to be hypnotized

by one word: cult. But here again his indignation is vain; and if we must find an excuse for him, perhaps it lies in his ignorance of the Latin tongue—as well as of French, incidentally. For him, "cult" has only one meaning: "adoration". On this, in the *Liber Accusationis*, he bases his reproach of having "violated the Gospel of Jesus Christ which obliges all creatures to 'adore God alone and worship none but him'." This is Jesus' answer to the devil who promised him glory and power "if you bow down and adore me".[6] Before hurrying to defend the rights of the only God against the one whom he makes out to be an adorer of man, why did he not consult a dictionary? *Cultus*, which comes from the verb *colere*, means *cura*, *diligentia*; it also means *veneratio*; we speak of cultivating letters, philosophy, justice, etc. There is also the cult of man, the cult of *humanitas* (which has nothing to do with Auguste Comte's religion); this cult, says an ancient writer, is proper to the cultivated man and is the office of wisdom. In Christian language the word takes on new and richer nuances, in harmony with the dogmas of creation and the Incarnation. *Cultus* is also *pietas*;

[6] Lk 4:8. The two words in Jesus' reply are προσκυνήσεις (*adorabis*) and λατρεύσεις (*servies*). The verb *servire* can be translated "to serve" or "to pay worship to" (Jerusalem Bible).

and we do not divinize man or adore the devil when we pay to our parents the homage of our filial piety.

Cultus gives us *cultor*, the approximate equivalents of which might be *studiosus*, *amator*, *custos*, *servator*; the word *admirator* can easily be joined with these; its main antonyms are *inimicus* and *contemptor*. All these various meanings exist in French, even though there is no noun corresponding with the word *cultor*. Of course, *cultus* can also have a "cultic" sense and in certain extreme cases might be equivalent to *adoratio*. But there is no more scandal (and much more reason) in speaking of the cult of man, or of admiration for man, than in professing a cult of, or admiration for, literature or tennis.

5. One remark of capital importance remains to be made. Although he selected from Paul VI's discourse (and isolated from its context) the passage which was to feed the fire of his indignation, the Abbé de Nantes did reproduce it most faithfully. By mentioning a two-line phrase, he provides us, with perfect honesty, the proof of the irrelevance of his criticism: "*The old story of the Samaritan inspired the Council's spirituality.*" He reads that sentence; he quotes it; but he does not see it. Such is the blindness produced by passion. Man who makes himself God, who wants to be the principle

and final norm of everything, who rises up "in his monstrous mien"—who is he really, in the Pope's eyes? In spite of the genuine progress of which he is so proud, man is only a poor wounded wayfarer, prostrate at the side of the road, about to die, upon whom the Council has learned from Christ to look with love. The Council did not wish to crush him under the weight of its anathemas; but it could hardly have been tempted to take him as its leader! Like the good Samaritan it bent over him, with all the greater pity since it could see in him his original nobility and beauty and even the conquests of his genius, disfigured by his wounds.[7] To serve man, every man, the Council proposed to him another kind of humanism, a different cult of man, the very kind that his Creator and Savior pledges him.[8]

Anathemas are more eloquent than quotations. They dwell longer in people's minds. And even

[7] Cf. St. Ambrose, whom Paul VI quoted previously and on whom he had commented more than once when speaking of "compassion" and "mercy": "For us, Christ is everything. If you need dressing for your wounds, he is the physician; if you are burning with fever, he is the fountain. If you fear death, he is life." "We are called", said the Pope on December 31, 1975, "to be the physicians of this civilization of which we dream. . . ." See other passages in Daniel Ange, *Paul VI, un regard prophétique* (Editions Saint-Paul, 1979), 56–62.

[8] "*Deus, qui humanae substantiae dignitatem mirabiliter condidisti, et mirabilius reformasti. . . .*"

among those with cultivated intellects, only a few
take time to read a rather long text with adequate
attention. Many, on the contrary, know of it only
what has trickled through interested or partisan
commentaries. From the Abbé de Nantes and some
others, public opinion retained only the condem-
nation of a pope who had dared to advocate
the Masonic worship of "Promethean man".
Thus "Clavel the paladin",[9] in the ardor of his
Catholicism and the brusque spontaneity of his
journalistic talent, one day allowed himself to be
deceived by a small group of clerics and to join his
voice with theirs.

On the other hand, there were some other
writers, apparently more equitable, who praised
Paul VI and the Council for their sympathy
towards mankind. But was this praise always
objective and disinterested? One can judge this
by what happened afterward. They too called
attention to "Promethean man", which was all
they mentioned; they too saw no further than
the expression of "sympathy"; they completely
skipped the *"old story of the Samaritan"* whose
generous charity they no doubt found not progressive enough for their taste.[10] Thanks to these
selective emphases and these omissions, both

[9] Fr. Bruckberger, *Lettre à Jean-Paul II, pape de l'an 2000*
(Stock, 1979), 139.

[10] We find this also in Six, *Le Courage de l'espérance*, 11–12.

Pope and Council became responsible for a vast movement of secularization, after which there was nothing easier, while continuing to exalt "the spirit of the Council", than to make the Pope contradict himself. When he firmly reasserted the Catholic faith, when he forgot that in the Church "authority should never again be unilateral", this was because he was reverting to the mentality of a preconciliar pontiff, guided by the "befuddled brains of obscurantist dogmaticians", as one journalist expressed it, with as little respect for the truth as for elegance of style.[11] He once more allowed "fear" to prevail over love and liberty. Hence there arose the danger of reviving an "intransigent Catholicism"; so tenacious does the old nightmare remain of a "monolithic absolute, lacking all tenderness", which would make any "pluralistic existence" impossible in the Church. So the conflict grew sharper "between the burning desire expressed at Vatican II for true liberty for Christians, following Christ who was free, and an intense fear and the consequent resolve to crush this new seed which was arising like the one that appeared at Pentecost".[12] How many similar statements have we not read in these last twelve

[11] Quoted by Six, ibid., 252.
[12] Ibid., 317 and 320.

years, from passionate defenders of the "Council" against a Pope who had not been slow in betraying it!

III

Then in 1978 Paul VI died, and after the brief pontificate of John Paul I came the election of John Paul II. This provided the occasion for new invectives, but in a different sense, against the Pope of the Council. "The Church", as the Abbé de Nantes wrote, "lived from December 7, 1965, until August 6, 1978, under the malediction of this impossible 'alliance between Christ and Belial', as St. Paul said (2 Cor 6:14–16)."[13]

Has that malediction come to an end? "We had hoped so until yesterday but not anymore." With his first encyclical the new Pope "claims the inheritance" of the Council and of Paul VI. He echoes the "fundamental dualism" of his predecessor,

> who inaugurated in the Church the CULT OF MODERN MAN, without for all that renouncing the worship of God . . . assigning to man, at the same time, two ultimate ends, two hares to be pursued

[13] Abbé Georges de Nantes, *La Contre-Réforme catholique au XXᵉ siècle* 141 (May, 1979): 1.

at once: ETERNAL SALVATION . . . and HUMANITY'S
LIBERATION. This is, in all truth, the faith of the
Catholic Church on the one hand, and on the
other, the Masonic ideal.[14]

A solemn protestation must be raised again, for
"it is not possible that a tradition of betrayal
should be established in the Church!" So here
comes another "anathema" launched against Paul
VI, this time for having dared, in his message to
the UN on October 4, 1970, "to ask for all,
without exception in regard to age, race, sex or
religion, the respect due to their human dignity
and the conditions needed to enjoy it". Faithfully
echoing the disastrous Council, he thereby completed the long descent "from the Gospel declaration of the dignity, the liberty, the rights of *Christian
man*, to those of *man*, mere man". He was thus
allowing himself to be swept along by "the
new humanism, which is resolutely lay", which
considers "man in himself" as "the source of
rights, the basis of his own dignity, the possessor
by nature of absolute liberty". Like the Council he
makes man a "son of earth, its god, the sovereign
and master of all things". Having "put to death
her rightful spouse, Jesus Christ", the Church was

[14] Ibid., 140 (April, 1979): 1–8: "He impudently divinizes
man."

now espousing "lay humanism", "to the acclamation of Freemasons, of all atheists and of all the wicked men on the planet".[15]

This may be sincere fanaticism, but it makes nonsense of logic! We merely need to observe that the two popes thus accused said something altogether different from what has been placed on their lips. Every reader who has not lost his mind will agree.

Five months later, a new attack on the memory of Paul VI came from another cleric, a man of great talent; and it must be admitted that the present state of the Church in France provided ample targets for his verve. We do not doubt that a genuine and deep attachment to the person of Jesus is, in the Reverend Father Bruckberger, the source of the anguish that pierces through his pamphleteer's temperament. But how could he fail to recognize that same attachment, that same burning passion, even if differently expressed, in the acts of Paul VI all through his pontificate, beginning with his allocution at the opening of the second session of the Council and his pilgrimage to the Holy Land? Nor do we doubt that Father Bruckberger's last piece of writing, the *Lettre à Jean-Paul II, pape de l'an 2000*, was inspired above

[15] Ibid., 141 (May, 1979): 2–10.

all by his love for the Church. When he tells us that a party took shape in her bosom, "on the occasion and under the pretext of the last Council, proposing purely and simply to change the Catholic religion, to change its substance discreetly but surely",[16] it seems to us he is merely stating an obvious fact for which many other proofs might be adduced. We might add that his adverb "discreetly" is by now largely ignored; but that, on the other hand, the immense majority of those who more or less followed that party did so unconsciously. Again, how could one fail to reject as he does, in speaking of faith, that indeterminate flight "into the shadowy and unbounded empire of ambiguity"[17]—even though it might be necessary to verify the applications of this. (One might also desire, in so serious a matter, fewer generalizations and more precise facts along with a different tone.) But it is harder to understand how, after deploring that Paul VI, that faithful and

[16] Bruckberger, *Lettre à Jean-Paul II*, 22; cf. 27–28, 56–57, 61–62, etc. The author speaks of a "conspiracy of technocrats", which impoverishes the phenomenon by trying to state it too precisely. We might add that we are far from seeing as "party men" all those with whom we cannot fully communicate in one and the same faith—something that makes us suffer.

[17] Ibid., 163.

indefatigable interpreter of Catholic tradition and
of the expression the Council gave of it, was not
listened to, he lays the responsibility for this on
the Pope's shoulders. Paul VI, he says, was "an
absent Father". His voice, when he did speak,
gave the impression of being that of a dead person
"in a posthumous broadcast"; or else it was like "a
lesson learned by rote", a ceremony "which he
went through like a docile pupil, somewhat after
the fashion in which the Queen of England reads
the 'Address from the Throne' ". Throughout the
thirteen years of his pontificate, "a time that
seemed to us interminable and during which the
Vicar of Christ was apparently plunged into an
enchanted sleep", we were left to the mercies of
"emptiness", "dizzy with absence".[18] Those to
whom he spoke could always pretend that they
had not heard anything. If he was not heeded, it
was because he did not seriously want to be. In the
"crucial case of the priesthood", for instance, he
deliberately "remained in an ambiguous position",
hoping thereby "to safeguard by any and all
means an external unity that only provisionally
camouflaged" the deep antagonisms.[19] Again,
if his encyclical *Humanae vitae* was "violently

[18] Ibid., 48–49.   [19] Ibid., 64–65.

resisted on all sides", this was simply due to the fact that "it was a timid encyclical and in the long run an encyclical that failed." He always "stopped halfway", bogged down in "false debates", and seemed to be "playacting in a shadow theater".[20]

Nothing could be more unjust. The author himself, if he rereads what he wrote and if, yielding to a praiseworthy impulse, he abandons a little of his haughtiness, will be obliged to admit this. For, as soon as he gets out of his own "shadow theater" and begins to speak like a realistic observer, he agrees, and even exaggerates somewhat in the other direction, that Paul VI "administered some very stiff warnings, some very severe rebukes" and even, "as it is said", could give some people a good dressing down.[21]

Still, the author of the *Lettre à Jean-Paul II* shows hardly more indulgence to Paul VI than the author of *La Contre-Réforme catholique au XXe siècle*. What follows will demonstrate this. But the tactics of the two writers (we are not using this

[20] Ibid., 120 and 124. These last expressions are cast in a negative form to show what John Paul II is not or does not do, in contrast (as everyone can understand) with what Paul VI was and did: "You cannot be accused of going only half way. . . . You are not made for pseudo-debates or the shadow theater. . . ."

[21] Ibid., 12–14.

word in a pejorative sense) are different; and because of this they sometimes contradict each other in the interpretation of the same passages. Whereas in April 1979 the Abbé de Nantes detected in the encyclical of John Paul II the same dualism and the same betrayal that he had discovered in the conciliar discourse of Paul VI and proceeded to anathematize both popes, in September Fr. Bruckberger compared them and found in them an absolute contrast. He could not find anything reprehensible in *Redemptor hominis* and declared himself to be full of hope:

> You place man in his ambiguous and irreducible destiny, which is unique. You do not speak of the "cult of man" for all that, because the context which the expression "cult of man" evokes for us, men living towards the end of the second millennium, is necessarily that of Hegel and of the "master thinkers": "Man is his own final end." It necessarily evokes the third temptation according to Matthew's Gospel and the definitive reply Jesus made to the devil: "The Lord God shalt thou adore and *him only shalt thou serve*."[22]

The author adds, alluding to the Christmas message of 1978: "You speak of the 'feast of man',

[22] Ibid., 127–28. One might observe that 1965 was not exactly "the end of the second millennium".

and that is something very different." Yes, no doubt it was; and this was obviously something more appropriate on Christmas. But Paul VI, too, often spoke of many other things besides this "cult of man". When one wishes to oppose one pope to another, it is not enough to notice that the latter does not limit himself, especially when the circumstances are totally different, to reusing the same words the former had used. The contrast invented here is all the more absurd because in his Christmas messages Paul VI himself had extolled that day as "the feast of life taken in its source": "O all ye men who hear us today, our joy is the greatest of all"; we are celebrating "a mystery of goodness which gives rise to rejoicing and to hope . . . in veins infected by sin and sorrow". On this day Christ came for each one of us; each one of us in our own individuality "is the person with whom he wants to be"; he came, "calling us by our names", and what happened once at Bethlehem "begins afresh today".[23] These words were pronounced at Christmas, 1972. Fr. Bruckberger rightly admires their almost literal reproduction in the Christmas message of 1978—but he does so as though we were finally hearing an entirely new voice: "If today we celebrate . . . the birth of

[23] Midnight Mass, Christmas 1972, at the steelworks in Taranto. Cf. the beautiful canticle in the Christmas message of 1971, etc.

Jesus, we do so to bear witness to the fact that every man is unique, absolutely special", because for God "man is always a unique being, absolutely singular . . . someone who is called and named by his own name."[24]

It was no doubt a good idea to note the strong emphasis that the new Pope placed on this word "singular", a word which is indeed pregnant with meaning. But it really was not necessary to add, by way of commentary and as though to disparage his predecessor: "Most Holy Father, you have just come to us . . . and from the first you stress . . . the singularity of each man born into this world. This is a good sign, an excellent and most significant sign. . . . Henceforth [men] will know that what the Church has to tell them is not nonsense. . . . That is something new!"[25]

We need not repeat here what we said above about the discourse given in 1965 and about the "cult of man", in reply to the identical accusations made by the Abbé de Nantes. Let us be satisfied with two simple remarks.

An expression which "necessarily" evokes an-

[24] Quoted by Bruckberger, *Lettre à Jean-Paul II*, 129.

[25] Ibid., 133. It is significant that in his speech at Puebla, John Paul II used the word "humanism", which Paul VI had also used and in the same sense: "In the presence of so many other humanisms", the Church proposes "the truth about man", the "complete truth about the human being".

other may do so either to approve the latter or to contradict it. Now, in the present case, the contradiction was explicit, insistent; it made up the substance of the talk; and one wonders how Fr. Bruckberger did not notice this. Of the many passages which contrast "man in relation to God as his center and his end" and "man who dares pretend to be the principle and the final norm of everything", Fr. Bruckberger has not remembered a single word. In the pacific and charitable tone adopted by the Pope as well as by the Council,[26] eager, without being unfaithful to the truth, to obey Christ "who taught us to consider love for our brothers as the distinctive sign of his disciples", he does not want to see (in the teeth of the evidence) anything but that grovelling before the world, so rightly stigmatized later by Jacques Maritain in speaking of a certain number of faithless interpreters. In the second place neither he nor the Abbé de Nantes (who at least cited the passage) nor Jean-François Six took into consideration, in the very passage they criticize, the significant reference to "*the old story of the Samaritan*". Yet this was a more immediate "context" than that of the "master thinkers"![27]

[26] *Gaudium et spes*, no. 28, 2–3.
[27] I cannot bring myself to reproduce here in their entirety

Father de Riedmatten, his fellow Dominican, has shown himself a more honest historian and a more careful interpreter. Concluding his "History of the Pastoral Constitution" with the discourse made on December 7, he remarks that by this discourse, *Gaudium et spes*, which had just been promulgated, "received at that very moment its first and most authoritative commentary". He very rightly chose as significant the passage that begins with the words: "The old story of the Samaritan was the model of the Council's spirituality. . . ."[28] In his analysis of that same talk, M. Jean Mouroux observed no less correctly that it was "above all *theocentric*, entirely built upon

the insulting words that follow. Still, the reader has a right to know them, along with those that went before them, if he wishes to understand my judgment. The author criticizes (Bruckberger, *Lettre à Jean-Paul II*, 141) "that man, placed on high, who with unpardonable superficiality affirmed that we Christians too, and we more than the rest, profess the cult of man. Poor wretch, how could he not have realized what kind of a gang he was associating himself with, what sinister companions he was walking with?" The author of a pamphlet challenging that of Fr. Bruckberger was satisfied to say in passing that the latter's judgment of Paul VI is "rather short-sighted".

[28] Cf. the collective work *L'Eglise dans le monde de ce temps, Gaudium et spes, commentaires du Schéma 13*, French trans. (Paris and Tours: Mame, 1967).

'the direct relationship with the living God' ". It presented to "modern man, taken up by feverish external activity, contemplation and communion with God" as "the principle which structures all human activity, the end which goes beyond all human means, which throws light into their depths . . . by purifying and organizing them and ranging them in due order". He also remarked that in his description of the double visage of this *modern* man, Paul VI had not in the least yielded to some sort of naive optimism, nor had he at all masked "everything in the human condition which is fearsome and terrifying". He recalled, finally, the opposition so strongly underscored by the Pope between the two "religions", that of "the God who made himself man" and that of "man who makes himself God".[29]

But unfortunately, the most objective and most serious commentaries are read only by a few people in libraries, and the texts which they analyze are read even less; whereas pamphlets

[29] Jean Mouroux, "Le Discours de Paul VI à la clôture du concile", in *Vatican II, l'Eglise dans le monde de ce temps*, Unam Sanctam 65c (Paris: Cerf, 1967), vol. 3, 195–200. It is in virtue of its theocentric *principle*, as Mouroux says, that the Council, contemplating the face of God as revealed in Jesus, received for its *special norm* fraternal charity, an attitude made explicit in this final discourse.

spread everywhere, and in troubled periods they mislead public opinion, sometimes for a long while. So we think it is our turn now, in considering one who during an extremely difficult time showed himself the faithful successor of Peter and the loyal disciple of their unique Master, to proclaim without any false modesty our indignation at the malignity shown by those who defame him and trample upon his corpse.

IV

The saints rise up "at the crossroads where the inner illumination of the mystery of the Cross is transformed into meaningful behavior towards their neighbor, after the fashion of the good Samaritan". Without having looked for it, we find that this remark made recently by Fr. Hans Urs von Balthasar perfectly explains the attitude and the thinking of Paul VI as he interpreted the Council. It also seems to me to describe most accurately the martyrdom that Paul VI had to undergo in the footsteps of the Crucified.

A year before the death of this Pope, in a radio broadcast on the program "Art and Faith", a priest, moved by this situation, gave expression to the wounded hearts of numberless faithful Catholics. "What makes me suffer", he said, "in my love for the Church and for the truly Holy Father whom Christ maintains at her head, Pope Paul VI, pilgrim of the faith, apostle of unity, is to see him martyred by so many calumnies, like his Master. . . ." He also expressed his sorrow at the thought that these calumnies, spread everywhere, were received in all innocence by so many people "who learn what he has said and done only through their newspaper, all of it twisted out of shape to make it more sensational, when it is not just simply and widely ignored".[30] Back in 1970, Fr. Jacques Loew had written: "They are stoning the Church in the person of the Pope, not with rocks, but with the projectiles called slogans. . . ."[31] And on September 16, 1979, a year after Paul VI's death, John Paul II himself, not content with having referred to him many times in his own teachings, compared "this great, humble man"[32] to the Apostle Paul, "crucified to the world" in the footsteps "of our Lord Jesus Christ", and more particularly to our Lord himself in his Passion:

> The cross has its own special interior dimension and Paul VI knew this dimension well. "Outrage"

[30] Canon Barbe, on Radio-Monaco (June 1977).
[31] Jacques Loew, retreat given at the Vatican in 1970.
[32] Cf. John Paul I (Aug. 27, 1978).

and "obloquy" were not spared him (cf. Is 50:6). He had to endure this as the master and the servant of truth; nor was his soul spared that sorrow and anguish spoken of by the Psalmist (Ps 116:3). . . . But during this extraordinary period of major changes following the Council, he was the rock, the foundation stone on which the Church was being built.[33]

After such a testimonial one should remain silent. May I be permitted, nevertheless, to add to it a few lines from an article which appeared in *L'Osservatore Romano* on June 21, 1978. I do this in a spirit of reparation, for *in spite of myself* I feel *linked* with some who are or were very close to me, one of whom has publicly surpassed the authors quoted in these pages in his affronts to Paul VI.

For fifteen years Pope Paul's hand has grasped the tiller. . . . With methodical and tenacious firmness, which has never ceased giving the lie to an equally stubborn legend, he has been guiding the bark of Peter. Of all that his detractors state, only one fact must be retained: the suffering that overcomes him at times and that he cannot disguise; but never does it break him or even slow his advance. In truth, we should regret it if this sign of humanity,

[33] John Paul II, homily at the Mass celebrated on the anniversary of the death of Paul VI. Cf. quotations in the Encyclical *Redemptor hominis*.

among so many others, were lacking to him, this trait of resemblance with Jesus. And what makes him even dearer to us is precisely the outrageous disparagement he meets with, not so much from the "world"—and certainly not from the vast majority of Christians, whether Catholics or not —but rather from those whose support he had every right to expect and count on.

Long ago (should we say only long ago?) people used to talk of "court theologians", those intellectuals who have never been absent from the circle surrounding all sorts of princes. If such people still exist today, whoever has his eyes open knows that he need not look for any around the chair of Peter. The all-powerful queen who distributes her favors is somewhere else. But the Christ who met with outrages is closer than ever to Peter. . . .

APPENDIX E

CONCERNING "THE SACRED"

Not long ago one might have read in a well known review that the idea of the "sacred" is not found in the New Testament. In fact, the word itself is found in 2 Tim 3:15—ἱερὰ γράμματα—not to mention the use of words like *sacerdos*, *sacramentum*, *sacrificium*. But this is more than a mere matter of words. It is certainly true that the New Testament, which is not a dictionary, contains no definition of the "sacred". A very learned author remarked long ago that the entire Book of Psalms contained no formal teaching about prayer. Still, one does not need to be very perspicacious, or to be an expert in the most demanding type of critical method, to notice pretty quickly that there is prayer in the Psalms and hence a good deal of "teaching by doing" about prayer. One might say something analogous about the "sacred". As an abstract concept it is hardly to be found in the New Testament, but it is there in reality, in act, which is certainly of greater value. One can see this for oneself by reading the first chapters of Mark, the earliest of our Gospels. One can see it again, to use only these examples, in the accounts of the Last Supper, in the Epistle to the Hebrews, in the sacramental symbolism of John's Gospel, etc. What is certain is that the "sacred", or the "sense of the sacred", which is natural to man, has undergone profound transformations in the course of history. One consequence of the revelation of the one God, the Creator, is the "demythologizing" of the world which we see taking place in the history of ancient Israel; but this "is absolutely not a desacralization. But we find a considerable transformation of the very idea of the sacred; it is restructured in relationship to the holiness of the one God. . . . In relation to paganism, the basis of sacrality undergoes a total change" (J. Grelot: "Le sens du sacré", in *Le Lien*, no. 119, October 1979, 3–5).[1]

One might add that the God of the Jews and the

[1] Cf. Claude Geffré in *Le Point théologique*, ed. C. Kannengiesser (Paris: Beauchesne, 1977), vol. 22: "Christianity is itself at the origin of a new sacredness. . . . This is why it is better to say that Christianity brought about a *metamorphosis* rather than a withering away of the sacred." Cf. 134, where he talks about the "ideology of secularization". See A. Vergote, ibid., 20–22, on "the enlightened clerics who joyously aid the desacralizing secularization of the Christian world". On the

Christians (and doubtless of many others too) is different from the "philosophers' God" (as Pascal understood that term), especially by reason of his sacred character.

The following essay, written by Fr. Michel Sales, S.J., does not seek to describe the various forms in which the sacred presents itself in the religious history of humanity but deals with discerning, in the light of God's word, the truly sacred element in every man.

H. L.

MAN IN THE PRESENCE OF THE TRULY SACRED AND OF THE PSEUDO-SACRED

1. Universality and Diversity of the Sacred

The history of religions shows that wherever men have lived, there has existed a sense of the sacred. In the presence of certain events in life, of certain objects, of certain beings, man experiences a feeling of fright, of religious awe (in Latin, *tremendum*), or of supernatural and adoring fascination (*fascinans*) which gives rise to certain forms of behavior by which, in a manner indissolubly

---

"transfer" of the sacred, see my *Images de l'abbé Monchanin* (Paris: Aubier-Montaigne, 1967), chap. 7, 67–76; Henri Cazelles, "Sacré et sacrifice", in *Communio* 3 (1980): 76–81.

spiritual and corporal, he expresses his acknowledgment of the sacred. The word *hierophany* (from
the Greek φαίνω: to show, to manifest; and ἱερός:
that which is sacred) applies to the places, objects,
persons and all the other realities through which
the sacred manifests itself to man, or in the
presence of which man experiences the sacred.
Now, as a specialist in the history of religions has
remarked: "It is certain that everything that man
has handled, felt, met with or loved could become
a hierophany."

We know, for instance, that taken by and large,

gestures, dances, children's games, toys, etc.,
have a religious origin; at one time they were
gestures and objects used in worship. We also know
that musical instruments, architecture, means of
transportation (animals, chariots, boats, etc.) were
in the beginning sacred objects or activities. Very
likely, no animal or plant exists which in the
course of history has not participated in this sort
of sacrality. We also know that all crafts, arts,
industries and techniques started with something
sacred, or at one time or another in their history
took on a cult value. This list might be continued
by the daily actions (rising, walking, running),
by the different kinds of work (hunting, fishing,
agriculture), by all the physiological acts (eating,
sex) and probably also by the basic words in each

language, and so on. Somewhere, at a given historical moment, each human group acting for itself has changed a certain number of objects, animals, plants, gestures, etc., into hierophanies; and it is highly probable that in the long run nothing escaped this transformation, which continued for tens of thousands of years of religious living.[2]

2. The Hiding of the Sacred Today

One often hears today that man has lost the sense of the sacred; in fact, what has really happened is that this sense has been *displaced* onto events, objects and persons to which our present-day world has given a quasi-sacred value. Think of the ceremonies surrounding certain sporting events, like the Olympic Games (the lighting of the flame which has been brought from afar; the "religious" attitude assumed during the performance of national anthems and the Olympic anthem, etc.). Remember the cult of personality paid in Russia and by all the militant communists in the world to the "little father of the people", Joseph Stalin, or more recently still to Mao Tze Tung in China or at the Sorbonne in May 1968.

[2] Mircea Eliade, *Traité d'histoire des religions*, new rev. ed. (Paris: Payot, 1974), 24.

Consider the masses of young people electrified by this famous singer or by that film actor. If one reflects on this it all testifies to man's invincible urge to find in this world some being, some reality to which he can devote himself body and soul in an attitude of adoration, admiration, self-renunciation and service.

So, the sacred has not suddenly disappeared in our day; but by being displaced it has in some sort *camouflaged* itself in unexpected shapes. In particular, the way "politics" has been overvalued in recent years is an excellent example of this, which was brought out by an atheist and materialistic sociologist, Claude Lévi-Strauss, when he observed that "nothing resembles more closely—from a strictly formal point of view—the myths of those societies which we call exotic or primitive than the political ideology of our own societies."[3]

3. The Real Problem: Distinguishing The Truly Sacred from the False, Aided by the Word of God

Man's innate sense of the sacred has not disappeared; one cannot even say that it has grown dim. It has found new objects; it has disguised itself. One must add, further, that most of the time it *goes*

[3] In *Esprit* (Nov., 1963), 643.

astray. Man sacralizes, "absolutizes" persons, objects and events which should not be treated in that way; and after a period of enthusiasm he finds himself alone, disappointed, with his broken idols in his hands. The real question, then, is not whether the sense of the sacred has diminished or disappeared but rather what makes man transform a reality of this world into something sacred for him, something which he places ahead of everything else, on which he spends his time and to which he even devotes himself wholly. Since there certainly is a *false* sacredness, the question is how to know whether a *true* one exists and where to find the truly sacred which alone deserves our inner attention, our respect and our religious submission.

From this point of view believers, both Jews and Christians, find in God's word an absolute and efficacious principle of judgment. In the first words of the Decalogue, God tells us: "Thou shalt not have strange gods before me" (Ex 20:3). In other words, there is no other God but God; he alone is holy, and consequently he alone, strictly speaking, is sacred for us, worthy of unreserved respect and absolute adoration from us. Everything else on the face of the earth is only a *means* to help us praise and serve God. Man himself is not, strictly speaking, a "sacred" being, in spite of what is often said of him. That is why, although making the second commandment obligatory like the first, Jesus does not give both of them the same contents (cf. Mk 12:28–34). He says, like the Torah, that one must love God with all one's heart, soul, mind and strength, whereas he specifies that we must love our neighbor *as ourselves* (not more than ourselves), that is to say, as a being which is infinitely prized in God's eyes but is not God and hence may not here below be loved, served or adored like God. For Christians, Christ alone is worthy of the same homage as God precisely because he is the Son of God, not in a metaphorical sense, but in absolute terms, as the Apostles proclaimed despite the objurgations of the highest religious authorities in the community of Jews to which they belonged. To the high priest and the Sanhedrin, who forbade them to preach in the name of Jesus, Peter and the Apostles replied: "We ought to obey God rather than men" (Acts 5:29).

The believer has at his disposal a sure criterion to distinguish the truly sacred from the false, for he is enlightened by God's historic revelation, inaugurated in the Old Testament and fully accomplished in Christ, in whose person God remains God even as he reveals himself, not only as close as possible to man, but as becoming man himself. Never before, on this point, did any human doctrine actually draw God and man closer than Christianity does; none was capable of doing so. God himself is the only one who could do it; any human invention is merely a dream, a fragile illusion. But nor was any doctrine ever so carefully preserved from the most horrible of all blasphemies: that since God had become man, this act of his should be profaned by supposing that God and man were actually the same.[4]

4. What is Truly Sacred in Every Man

a. His conscience

But in addition there is in man, in every man whether he calls himself a "believer" or not, a double testimonial, and as it were a double presence of the *truly sacred*: in his body and in his spirit.

The first testimonial, an undeniable and universal one showing that in man there is something truly sacred, is man's moral conscience, i.e., the

[4] Soren Kierkegaard, *Traité du désespoir*, Idées (Paris: Gallimard, 1949), 225. All that we say of the person of Jesus Christ, the Word of God made flesh, applies analogically to his real presence in the Eucharist and to his "mystical body", i.e., the Church, considered as an eschatological reality, who has Christ for her head and those who are sanctified for her members.

principle by which man cannot help recognizing the difference between good and evil and which prevents him from calling evil good and good evil. "Conscience", wrote Newman,

> is a personal guide; I make use of it because I must make use of myself. I cannot think with another man's mind any more than I can breathe with his lungs. Conscience is for me the closest instrument of knowledge that I have at hand. It is given to me even as it is to my neighbors. Everyone bears it within his bosom; it needs nothing else but itself; it transmits admirably to each one in particular the instructions he needs most for his individual life. It is practically adapted to all social classes and levels, to the great as well as to the humble, to young and old, to men and women. It does not depend on books, on learned seductions, scientific knowledge or philosophy.[5]

There is no situation, however horrible, despairing or desperate it may be, in which conscience cannot play its role, witnessing to man's indefectible dignity. Many recent examples of this kind come to us from the material and spiritual

[5] John Henry Cardinal Newman, *Grammaire de l'assentiment*, quoted in *Oeuvres philosophiques de Newman* (Paris: Aubier-Montaigne, 1945), 47. Cf. "Lettre au duc de Norfolk", in *Textes newmaniens*, trans. B.-D. Dupuy (Brussels and Paris: DDB, 1970), vol. 7, chap. 5, 236–62.

desolation of what A. Solzhenitsyn named "the Gulag Archipelago". One chapter in his book *The First Circle* was entitled: "Man has only one conscience". This statement, writes a specialist in Soviet literature,

> sums up in a few words the most essential discovery made in these last fifteen years in the U.S.S.R. It is true for the individuals who, thanks to it, have emerged from their isolation; it applies also to an entire society which had forgotten it, and it reflects a deep reversal of opinion. It is not by chance that the post-Stalin literature, even after official editing, which means having passed the narrow gates of official censorship, puts preoccupations of the ethical order in the first rank.
>
> If one takes a writer like Bykov, whose works, published in the famous review *Novy Mir*, are based on incidents that occurred during the last war, the center of interest is the moral attitude of the characters. One of his recent stories is about a partisan, Sotnikov. Wounded, he is captured along with one of his comrades by the local pro-German police. While his fellow prisoner offers them his services to save his skin, Sotnikov refuses that solution. He is condemned to death. Here are his thoughts in the presence of the gibbet: "No; indeed not; death does not solve anything and does not justify anything. . . . All that remained in his power was to leave this world with a clear

conscience, with the dignity that belongs to a man. That was the last favor, the sacred luxury that life offered him as a reward."

This reaction was not based on a belief in the next world. It rather resembles Stoicism; but it implies the existence of an unchallengeable moral law, the observance of which makes man all the greater. Solzhenitsyn formulated that law in this way, in the words of a peasant, Spiridon: "The wolf-dog is right; the cannibal is wrong." It is in the depths of one's being that one listens to it or refuses it. That choice is made without harangues or orations; it can be dramatic in the degree to which death or life depends on it. If one follows this inner voice, it is not only to exalt in oneself the sentiment of one's own dignity but equally out of a concern not to harm others.[6]

After this, one understands that Cardinal Newman could say of conscience that it was, in every man, like "the natural vicar of Christ".[7]

---

[6] Hélène Zamoyska, "Réflexions sur les problèmes de l'intériorité en URSS.", in *Axes* (Feb.–March, 1973), 61. The entire article deserves to be quoted. In fact, the author shows further on how this moral conscience, thus reborn, is a sure guide for finding God.

[7] *Certain Difficulties Felt by Anglicans in Catholic Teaching*; French trans. in John Henry Cardinal Newman, *Pensées sur l'Eglise*, Unam Sanctam 30 (Paris: Cerf, 1956), 130. The entire admirable passage dealing with the relationship between the

b. Modesty

There is a second witness to the truly sacred residing in man's body, one to which we cannot be too attentive: *modesty* (or, in its negative form, shame). This sentiment, which is entirely lacking in animals, not only offers no social interest; it is rather an embarrassment that overcomes man in spite of himself and sometimes paralyzes him. Universally observed in all human societies, where it can assume very diverse forms (clothing, though it be reduced to a simple loincloth, is one of its major symptoms), this sense of modesty is not only a distinctive note which, for an external observer, distinguishes and separates man from the rest of the animal world. By it man really sets himself apart from the whole of material nature, both that which surrounds him and that which is proper to him.

> When he feels shame for his own natural tendencies and the functions of his organism, man by that fact shows that he is not only *this* material being but that he is also something else, something superior.
>
> In the psychological act of modesty, he who

---

pope's authority and individual conscience is well worth reading: 129–32. On the dignity of the moral conscience, see also *Gaudium et spes*, no. 16.

feels shame separates himself from that of which he is ashamed. Now, material nature cannot be estranged from, or external to, itself; hence, if I feel shame for my material nature, I prove by that very fact that nature and myself are not identical. It is precisely at the moment when man falls under the influence of a material function of nature and is made one with it that his distinctive particularity and his inner independence express themselves in his feeling of modesty, in which and by which he considers material life as something different from himself, something foreign to him, something which must not rule him.[8]

The reader may find it strange that I am advocating here a sentiment which in today's world seems to be in such disfavor, and even directly contradicted. Just recently, could we not see on the newsstands a pornographic magazine which went so far as to take as its title one of the terms by which we designate God, "The Absolute"? Let us not be deceived. As Soloviev very correctly stated long ago, "intentional, exaggerated immodesty, an immodesty raised to the level of a religious principle, very obviously presupposes the existence of modesty." If any man or group of men simply lacked all sense of modesty (supposing that

[8] W. Soloviev, *La Justification du bien* (Paris: Aubier-Montaigne, 1939), 31–32.

such a case could exist), this would no more invalidate the universality of this distinctive sign of humanness than the fact that some children are born dumb invalidates the universality of spoken language.

In a remarkable book,[9] Fr. Gaston Fessard (1897-1978) showed that

> on the level of natural and human history, modesty is, in fact, an *essential* form of affectivity, so universal and so profound that while education or "culture" can no doubt sharpen it or weaken it, they can neither create nor destroy it. Now this specifically human sentiment, innate and basic, governs all human relationships from the most intimate carnal intercourse between the sexes to the most spiritual contacts which people establish among themselves. Its function is to prepare, to promote, to judge and to correct the expression of love, of personal reciprocity which, in the last analysis, is what is sought in and by all inter-human relationships.

[9] G. Fessard, *La Dialectique des Exercices spirituels de saint Ignace de Loyola*, 2 vols., Théologie 35 and 66 (Paris: Aubier-Montaigne, 1956 and 1966). This is a rather difficult work. The study on modesty is in the second volume, 127–256. See Max Scheler, *La Pudeur* (Paris: Aubier-Montaigne, 1952). The latter book also inspired a few pages in Cardinal Wojtyla's *Amour et résponsabilité* (Paris: Société d'éditions internationales, 1965), 162–79.

But modesty, by its absolute irreducibility, is something much more. It is, inserted into the most intimate fibers of the human body, "the presence of the natural desire to see God which is revealed to man from the first awakening of his personal conscience, from the initial point of his liberty." It enlightens man on the "nature" of his actual, *historical existence*, the fruit of a sinful liberty, and the impassable chasm (barring a new divine grace, a new gift, the gift of pardon) which separates him from the *essence* of his nature, from the Totality of being to which he aspires. Modesty is the condition for the *human* rapport between man and man, and no less so for the relationship between man and God; if it is, as Scheler remarks, "*the moral conscience* of human love", engraved in our biological nature, we will *a fortiori* find it present at the heart of the movement by which man, created in the image of God "who is love" and excluded by sin from intimacy with the Absolute, effectively relearns the love of God who is the All of his being and his will. Hence it is surprising that modesty, "which covers the entire field of human affectivity", governs all the stages of each person's spiritual life.

Fr. Fessard thus gives us a sort of typology of the essential social forms that modesty can assume, filial, conjugal, paternal, maternal, and of their correlative role in the pedagogy of love, of the divine ἀγάπη, the being and essence of the trinitarian life that every man is called to achieve, even here below, in his relationships with others.

Conclusion

One may say, if one wishes, that man has lost the sense of the sacred, provided one specifies: of the *truly* sacred. For in the history of mankind the *false* sacred has never ceased multiplying.[10] That was what the Bible called *idolatry*, i.e., the tendency, innate in man as a consequence of Adam's sin, to confer on created things, objects or persons an *excessive value* (even an absolute value) to such an extent that they rivalled God in his heart, God who alone is absolutely "holy". This is not something that began recently. But no matter how badly it has deviated, the ineradicable tendency of man to manufacture *pseudo*-sacred things still bears witness to the *truly* sacred in the measure in which the one who pretends to rid himself entirely of the sacred cannot do so without believing absolutely in his own attempt, thus making an idol of it. So that the most militant atheist is still only an idol

[10] Cf. A. Vergote in *Le Point théologique*, 22: "The process of desacralization . . . ends up by returning us to a savage sacrality. . . ." [H. L.]

worshipper who, as Origen said, prefers to relate to anything at all rather than to God his indestructible conviction of the existence of the only truly sacred.

Even when lost, the truly sacred is not far from any of us. It is not outside of us; it is *enshrined* in us by our moral conscience and our physical modesty. Anyone who makes himself ever more aware of their double and discreet testimony will find that his apprehension of God will revive in the same proportion and with it the sense of the truly sacred.

Michel Sales, S.J.
Feb. 17, 1979[11]

[11] Extract from the bulletin *Le Lien* 117 (April, 1979).